EYEWITNESS TO REDEMPTION:

FINDING REFUGE IN
GOD'S REDEEMING LOVE

Ruth

EYEWITNESS TO REDEMPTION:
FINDING REFUGE IN
GOD'S REDEEMING LOVE

Ruth

Mindy Ferguson

AMG Publishers, Inc. | amgpublishers.com

Eyewitness Bible Studies
Eyewitness to Redemption: Ruth, Finding Refuge in God's Redeeming Love
Copyright © 2023 by Mindy Ferguson
Published by AMG Publishers, Chattanooga, Tennessee 37421 (www.amgpublishers.com).

ISBN: 978-161715-594-9 (Paperback)
First Printing—March 2023

Cover design by Jonlin Creative, Pekin, IL
Editing by Marissa Wold Uhrina, Eden Prairie, MN
Interior design and typesetting by PerfecType, Nashville, TN

Printed in the United States of America

This study is dedicated to:

*My mother, Elizabeth Ruth, who worked hard all her days
and passed from this life into the eternal refuge of her Redeemer
a few weeks after the completion of this study.*

CONTENTS

Week 1: Relevant Reflections

Defining the Times. 1

Lingering Temptations. 5

Subverting the King 9

A Desolate Decade 13

Personal Application 16

Week 2: Exemplifying Kindness

Loyalty Returned 21

Bittersweet Reunion 25

Gleaning Favor. 29

A Man of Standing 33

Personal Application 36

Week 3: A Weighty Proposal

The Weight of Generosity 41

Character Amid Hard Times 45

A Thoughtful Plan 49

Seeking Coverage 53

Personal Applicatin 57

Week 4: Defining Refuge

Refuge Means Security 61

Refuge Means Provision 65

Refuge Means Peace 69

Refuge Means Mercy 72

Personal Application 76

Week 5: Judicious Decisions

Dawning Providence 81

The Wait 85

Unsandaled Mr. So-and-So 89

Building a Legacy 92

Personal Application 95

Week 6: Redemption

The Wedding 101

Lineage of a Son 105

Behold A New Life 109

Under His Wings 113

Redeeming Love 117

Notes 121

Additional Eyewitness series resources can be found at Mindyferguson.net.
Including: videos, leader's guides, and free handouts

Week 1

Relevant Reflections

Defining the Times

In those days Israel had no king; everyone did as they saw fit.

JUDGES 21:25

*T*he book of Ruth conveys a heart-rending story of redemption. As we will see in the coming weeks, Ruth and her mother-in-law, Naomi, experienced God's providential care and found refuge in His redeeming love. There is notably little information available about the setting in which this story unfolds, but after researching several sources, it seems the events of this anonymously written book took place sometime between 1100 and 540 BC. I must admit, the researcher in me was disappointed with that lengthy and uncertain time frame. However, my chronological Bible places the story between chapters twelve and thirteen of Judges.[1] If that placement is accurate, the events recorded in the book of Ruth occurred around 1060 BC. We will use that date and focus our study today on the information Scripture tells us about the setting for Ruth's story. I pray you experience the joy of discovery and the sweetness of God's presence as you read and study His Word through the pages of this workbook. Take a moment to pray that for yourself before you begin.

Let's begin our journey together by reading Ruth 1:1. Note everything you learn about the setting of Ruth's story:

_____

_____

About 400 years before the "days when the judges ruled," God delivered the Israelites from slavery in Egypt. They were a grumbly bunch of refugees who let fear weaken their faith. Because of their disbelief, they wandered in the wilderness for forty years before God eventually led them into the Promised Land of Canaan. During the conquest, the Israelites' commander was a faithful warrior named Joshua. After many battles, God's people were able to conquer the Canaanite inhabitants and took possession of the land. God then asked Joshua to distribute territory to each of the Israelite tribes. It was a time of great victory and celebration for God's people. Years later, when Joshua neared the end of his life, he gathered the people of Israel together to bid them farewell, to remind them of the success God had provided for them as they conquered the land, and to warn them about the importance of remaining devoted to their Lord.

Joshua's words will help us better understand the context of Ruth's story, so let's pretend we are sitting among the Israelites and take note of some of the highlights from Joshua's farewell address.

Please read Joshua 23:1–13.

According to verse 3, who fought on Israel's behalf? _____

Each of the twelve Israelite tribes were allotted territory in the Promised Land. Although nations had been conquered and the land distributed, there were still pockets of people from other nations living within the Israelite territories.

What warning did Joshua issue to the Israelites regarding those lingering foreigners (v. 7)?

_____

_____

What did Joshua urge the people to do "very careful[ly]" after his death (v. 11)?

_____

According to verses 12–13, what would happen if the Israelites allied themselves with the lingering people groups and intermarried with them?

1). God would no longer _____

2). The foreigners would become _____

Joshua's warning was clear. To avoid consequences, the Israelites were urged to develop a deep love for God and instructed to avoid worshiping the idols of the people from other nations. The generation of God's people who attended Joshua's farewell address were indeed careful to love the Lord and serve Him throughout Joshua's lifetime. Sadly, the same cannot be said of the generations that followed. Please read Judges 2:6–13.

According to verse 10, what was significantly different about the next generation of Israelites?

_____

Think about the scenario described in verse 10 for a moment. What had the Israelites of Joshua's day apparently failed to do?

_____

Parents cannot control the decisions their children make as adults; however, it is imperative that we, as followers of God, share the truths of God's Word with our children and grandchildren, as well as communicate our personal stories of God's faithful provision, protection, and goodness. On the lines below, list the names of people in the generation following yours (regardless their ages) with whom you have influence:

_____

_____

Take a moment right now to reflect on a personal experience when you were convinced God fought for you or provided for you in some tangible way. Describe the scenario in one sentence:

_____

Later this week, you will be given an opportunity to write a short summary of your experience and then share your story with someone of the next generation. Keep this assignment in mind throughout the week, and ask God to provide an opportunity for you to share.

For now, let's see how God responded to the faithless generation we just read about. Please read Judges 2:14–19.

Write the last sentence of verse 15: _____

What did the Lord do despite their lack of faith and stubborn rebellion (v. 16)?

_____

During the "days when the judges ruled," the people of Israel were continually tempted to worship the false gods of the people from other nations who were living among them. The Israelites intermarried with them and, as predicted, worshipped the various false gods that dominated those cultures. As a result, Israel was defeated in battles against those nations and repeatedly fell into periods of great distress. God would then raise up judges to save Israel from the oppression of their enemies, but as soon as a judge would die, the nation would once again fall into the same state of rebellion and decline (or worse!) until God raised up the next judge. The cycle occurred repeatedly throughout the book of Judges.

To close today's lesson, let's allow Scripture to provide a fitting summation of the "days when the judges ruled." Write Judges 21:25 on the lines below:

_____

_____

Sadly, when our descendants look back on our current times, I suspect our days might be described with similar words. Continue thinking about your story of God's faithfulness (we will call it a God story) that you will share with someone of the next generation. Who knows—God just may spare that younger person some future days of great distress because of your faithfulness to share your faith.

WEEK ONE DAY TWO

Lingering Temptations

Do not associate with these nations that remain among you; do not invoke the names of their gods or swear by them. You must not serve them or bow down to them.

JOSHUA 23:7

*I*n our last lesson, we learned a little about the setting in which our story from the book of Ruth unfolds. Sadly, although God had rescued His people from slavery in Egypt and enabled them to take possession of their Promised Land, they were continually tempted to worship the gods of the idol-worshiping people groups living among them. In response to Israel's rebellion, the Lord allowed them to be defeated in battles. As a result, the Israelites often found themselves in a state of oppression in their own homeland, prompting them to cry out to God. He would then mercifully send a judge to save them, and Israel would return their devotion back to God for a time. That repeated cycle of rebellion defined the "days when the judges ruled."

Before we move forward with new material, read Judges 2:16–19 again and note how God responded to the distressed cries of His people (v. 18):

_____

_____

Now read Psalm 106:34–45, which provides another recap of the situation in Israel during the time of the judges. What horrific Canaanite worship practice did the Israelites participate in according to verses 37–38?

_____

_____

According to verse 43, how often did God deliver His people from their oppressors, and how did the Israelites respond?

_____

_____

According to verse 45, what prompted God to relent from punishing His people, despite their evil behavior and rebellion?

_____

On the lines below, write the description of God recorded in Jonah 4:2.

_____

_____

The Israelites were God's covenant people, and He intended for them to enjoy rest and prosperity in the Promised Land. They were commanded to eliminate the temptation to worship false gods by driving out the foreign people groups living in their land. They should have been committed to their Lord, and they should have served Him faithfully. Instead, they refused to heed the warnings from their former leader, Joshua. They became imitators of the depraved culture of the lingering inhabitants of their land. God's people sank into such a state of rebellion that they even sacrificed their own sons and daughters as they worshiped the false gods of the Canaanites.

> The Israelites were God's covenant people . . .

I must say, the concept of sacrificing a human being as part of worship is appalling. I find myself wondering how the people could have declined into such a depraved state of mind and heart that they could sacrifice their own children to some lifeless, fictitious god. However, I do understand that people are influenced by the culture in which they live. I imagine the decline was a gradual process. The practices of the Canaanites probably slowly crept into their daily routines.

To seek some sort of relatability to the situation in Israel, take a moment to list some of the ways Christians today have been influenced by our culture:

_____

_____

_____

What does 1 Corinthians 15:33 tell us about the influence of people with whom we associate?

_____

Corrupted character is an understatement when considering the acts of God's people during the "days when the judges ruled," but the principle certainly applies. We are influenced by the people around us. Look again at Ruth 1:1. What agricultural circumstance prompted the family living in Bethlehem to relocate to Moab?

_____

Now read Deuteronomy 11:10–17. According to verse 12, who is it that cares for the land of Israel and continually watches over it?

_____

What did the Lord promise to do if His people faithfully loved the Lord and served Him while living in the Promised Land (vv. 13–15)?

_____

In addition to being defeated in battles, what other consequence did the Lord tell His people (through Moses) would result if they allowed themselves to be "enticed to turn away and worship other gods" (v. 17)?

_____

Now read Deuteronomy 11:18–21. Reflecting on what we learned in yesterday's lesson, how might the famine described in Ruth 1:1 be a consequence of Israel's failure to teach their children to know the Lord and understand all He had done for them?

The Canaanite people in that period believed the false god Baal was the owner of the land and controlled its fertility.[2] Their religion taught that the sexual union of Baal with his mother, Asherah, caused the soil to become fertile. "The Canaanite religion was based on a form of sympathetic magic" in which a priest represented Baal and women in the community represented Asherah.[3] It does not take much imagination to grasp the kind of depraved activities that surrounded the "sympathetic magic" that was prevalent in the worship of Baal and Asherah. Sadly, God's people were influenced greatly by the lingering temptation to trust in these wicked practices for their food supply rather than relying on the true God of Israel to watch over the land and keep His promises.

Read Ruth 1:1–2. Interestingly, this family's city of residence, Bethlehem, means "House of Bread."[4] The people in Israel had continually succumbed to the temptation to trust in false gods of their culture for their food supply rather than trusting God to provide for their needs and fill their houses with bread and sustenance. It is not a stretch to assume that Israel was in a period of rebellion when the famine mentioned in verse 1 ravaged their homeland and Elimelek decided it was time to move to more fertile soil.

Where did Elimelek, Naomi, and their two sons move to escape the famine?

The lingering temptation to worship the gods of the Canaanites took its toll on the entire nation of Israel. The book of Ruth gives us a glimpse into the personal journey of one family during this dark period in the "days when the judges ruled." We have a little more background information to study before we delve into the heart of this family's story; we will spend tomorrow's lesson doing just that. For now, spend the rest of today prayerfully considering how our current culture has tempted you to compromise your convictions or has drawn your heart away from a wholehearted devotion to our Lord. Make some notes on the lines below. (It's okay to write in code, just in case someone else happens to read your answers.)

WEEK ONE | DAY THREE

Subverting the King

And they went to Moab and lived there.

RUTH 1:2B

*E*limelek's family endured a famine in their country, and their hometown, named House of Bread, sorely lacked that grain-dependent sustenance. The scenarios are quite different, but I cannot help but wonder if the lack of grain in Israel spurred similar irrational behavior among the Israelites to what we witnessed from people during the toilet paper shortage of the COVID-19 pandemic. Typically rational, peaceful people were so desperate that armed officers had to guard toilet paper aisles in many of America's grocery stores. Desperate circumstances can breed some pretty irrational behavior, and for the Israelites, a famine did not just threaten their convenience and comfort, their shortage threatened their well-being and possibly even their survival.

What irrational behavior did you witness (or even display) during the early stages of the COVID-19 pandemic that might provide some insight into the behavioral climate of Israel at the opening of the book of Ruth?

_____

_____

_____

Whatever the scenario, Elimelek decided the situation was dire enough to pack up his family and head east to the region of Moab. A large part of the land in Moab was fertile and usually received adequate rain.[5] With the widespread famine in Israel, we can assume Elimelek's family set out for this new territory with the hopes of a more stable food supply and perhaps a less desperate community. However, the nation of Israel had some interesting history with the Moabites that made Elimelek's destination a somewhat questionable choice.

If you are familiar with the Old Testament story of Sodom and Gomorrah, you probably remember Abraham's nephew, Lot. As God rained down burning sulfur on Sodom and Gomorrah, Lot's family fled for the hills. Sadly, Lot's wife was forever preserved as a pillar of salt because she looked back to mentally preserve the memory of Sodom, despite God's warning not to do so. After making their way to safety, Lot and his two daughters set up house in a mountain cave. It was in that barren, cold, uncomfortable dwelling that Lot's son, Moab, was conceived.

Please read Genesis 19:30–38 and note the circumstances of Moab's birth.

_____

_____

The despicable scene in the cave was certainly not Moab's fault. He could have risen above his heritage. However, based on Scripture's description of the Moabite culture, it seems depravity continued to define the family's legacy. Interestingly, tensions were high between the Israelites and the Moabites.

The Lord outlined some worship guidelines for the Israelites in Deuteronomy 23:3–6. What additional information do you learn about the descendants of Moab from these passages?

_____

_____

What was the result of Balaam's attempt to curse Israel (v. 5)?

_____

Not only had the Moabites failed to provide food or water to the Israelites after their exodus from Egypt, but they had attempted to place a curse on Israel. In a continued effort to understand the history between the people of Israel and the people of Moab, let's briefly read about the circumstances surrounding the Moabites' attempt to curse Israel.

Please read Number 22:1–6.

What reason did the king of Moab give for his attempted cursing of Israel?

_____

Sadly, the Israelites' encounter with the Moabites took an even more grievous turn. Now read Numbers 25:1–3 and note what you learn about the Israelites' interaction with the Moabite women.

_____

_____

Sexual immorality was rampant in Moab just as it was prevalent in the cultures of the foreign people living among the Israelites in the Promised Land. But the Moabites' disdain for the people of Israel caused constant conflict. To better comprehend the status of their relationship during the "days when the judges ruled" (Ruth 1:1), let's read about one more important incident in Israel's history with Moab.

Please read Judges 3:12–30.

Who gave the king of Moab power over Israel (v. 12)? _____

How long was Israel subject to King Eglon (v. 14)? _____

Summarize the encounter between King Eglon and Ehud below.

_____

_____

_____

_____

The vivid aspects of this story are evidence that God does not spare us the grisly details from the history of His people.

Israel repeatedly turned to false gods of neighboring cultures and found themselves "subject to" their enemies. Then when they were once again in a state of oppression and distress, they would cry out to God for help. The process of overcoming their enemies was, at times, gruesome and can be uncomfortable for us to read about. However, the details serve as evidence that freedom and victory did not come without some intense physical battles during Old Testament times, and do not come without some intense spiritual battles in these New Testament times. Throughout Israel's history, whenever God's people turned away from Him, some gruesome battles were necessary for them to have victory once again over their enemies.

Moab was certainly an interesting relocation choice for Elimelek's family. Although grain was probably more prevalent in Moab, immorality was also widespread. God had warned his people not to worship alongside the Moabites (Deuteronomy 23:3), but Elimelek seemed to be more focused on his family's nutritional needs than their spiritual nourishment as he led his family east to Moab.

Interestingly, Elimelek's name means "God is King."[6] When God is king in our hearts, our choices reflect His lordship; our actions reflect faith. We cannot know Elimelek's thoughts or motives, but I suspect his decision to move his family to Moab was fueled by fear and the uncertainty of his times. Rather than relying on the One who provides "rain from heaven" and keeps His eyes on the land of Israel "from the beginning of the year to its end" (Deuteronomy 11:11–12), Elimelek did what he saw fit in order to provide for his family. I'd like to suggest Elimelek's decision to leave his homeland for what he hoped would be greener pastures reflected the attitude of the nation of Israel at the time: "In those days Israel had no king; everyone did as they saw fit" (Judges 21:25).

> When God is king in our hearts, our choices reflect His lordship; our actions reflect faith.

The hard truth is, when we do as we see fit rather than seeking God for guidance and trusting Him for our provision, we subvert God's authority and, in essence, put ourselves in the place of King over our lives.

Jesus is the King of kings and the Lord of lords. Any time we attempt to take control of our path, we subvert His Lordship and crown ourselves king or queen. That crown was never meant to be ours, and we can expect some tumultuous times ahead whenever we try to wear it.

WEEK ONE · DAY FOUR

A Desolate Decade

*After they had lived there about ten years, both Mahlon and Kilion also died,
and Naomi was left without her two sons and her husband.*

RUTH 1:4B–5

The period of the judges spanned over four hundred years, and the Moabites were not Israel's only enemies. The cycle of rebellion, repentance, and returning continued throughout "the days when the judges ruled." Elimelek's family decided to move to Moab about three hundred years after Ehud's gruesome slaughter of the Moabite king, Eglon.[7]

If you recall from our Day One lesson, *The Narrated Bible in Chronological Order*[8] places the date of the story we are studying around the thirteenth chapter of Judges.

Please read Judges 13:1, and circle the stage of Israel's rebellious cycle during the book of Ruth:

REBELLION   REPENTANCE   RETURNING

As our story unfolds, Israel was probably in the throes of a forty-year period of oppression from the Philistines. According to Ruth 1:1, how long did the family intend to stay in Moab?

Elimelek had intended to stay for a while in Moab and then return to his hometown of Bethlehem when the famine was over. As he prepared to leave Israel, Elimelek probably leased out his family's land until he planned to return. We cannot know all the preparations Elimelek took or the thoughtful discussions that occurred as he made the decision to move to Moab; however, as an Israelite man, Elimelek's preparation certainly should have included prayer and reflection on the Law of Moses, also called the Torah (the first five books of our Old Testament), which was a central part of his faith.

Let's look at a few passages from these books that address the source of the Israelites' security and sustenance.

According to Genesis 2:4, who created the earth? _____

Read Leviticus 26:3–5. What did God say He would do if His people faithfully followed His commands?

_____

According to Deuteronomy 28:2–6, what specific blessings could the Israelites enjoy if they obeyed the Lord?

_____

What truth from Deuteronomy 31:8 might have encouraged Elimelek as he and his family endured the famine in Israel?

_____

House of Bread was barren, but I have to wonder if Elimelek's heart may have been a bit barren of God's Word as well. Off the hungry family of four went toward the land they believed would bring the security and sustenance they were seeking. Sadly, as the family headed east to escape the famine, Elimelek and Naomi had no idea their journey to Moab would yield far greater losses than the lack of grain in Bethlehem.

Now read Ruth 1:3–5.

What happened shortly after the family moved to Moab (v. 3)?

_____

Elimelek and Naomi were real human beings, and Elimelek's death after the family had recently moved away from their friends and the familiarity of their hometown must have been distressing to Naomi and the boys. The devastating loss came at a time when the newly single mother and her two boys were isolated from the community that would have surrounded them with support as they grieved.

Think back to a time when you experienced a personal loss. The scenario could have been the death of a family member; a job loss; or even an injury or illness that hindered your physical strength, mobility, or independence. Whatever the situation, note below how friends and family members supported and comforted you as you grieved. (If, like Naomi, you lacked support, note how isolation intensified your grief.)

_____

_____

_____

How does that personal experience help you better understand the intensity of grief Naomi and her boys probably experienced when Elimelek died just after their move to Moab?

_____

_____

Naomi was left to navigate life in a foreign land without her husband. Her sons, Mahlon and Kilion, grew into men in Moab, and I suspect they did their best to make Moab feel like home. In fact, both sons married Moabite women. What were the names of their wives (v. 4)?

_____ and _____

According to Ruth 1:5, what happened to Mahlon and Kilion?

_____

Within a decade of arriving in Moab, Naomi had lost her husband and both her sons. Naomi, Ruth, and Orpah shared the common reality of life without a husband or children. In ancient Israel, a widow was unable to inherit her husband's money or land. When an Israelite man died, ownership of his family's land would then transfer to his oldest son. Sadly, when both of Naomi's sons died, so did ownership of property and her source of financial support.

Interestingly, Jewish rabbinic tradition considered Ruth to be the daughter of the Moabite king Eglon, whose gruesome murder we read about in our previous lesson.[9] There were probably too many years between these events to make that feasible, but Ruth may have been a descendant of that Moabite king. Whatever Ruth's heritage, without a husband, she did not appear to have access to wealth or provision. Naomi, Ruth, and Orpah were not just grief stricken after the loss of their husbands, these three widowed women instantly became poor. They were tragically plunged into desperate circumstances in Moab. Read the passages below and note what you learn about God's attitude toward widows such as Naomi, Ruth, and Orpah?

Exodus 22:22–23 _____

Psalm 68:5 _____

Psalm 146:9 _____

During her decade in Moab, Naomi had lost her husband, her children, and her financial support. The widows of her deceased boys were the only family she had left. She had come to Moab in search of sustenance and security. A decade later she became keenly aware that she was completely dependent on God alone for her survival.

Amid her season of loss and grief, Naomi received word of changes back in her homeland. According to Ruth 1:6, what had occurred back in Israel?

_____

The desolate decade ended as the three widows began making hopeful preparations for a relocation back in Israel. As we close our study today, the ending words of Psalm 30:5 remind me that desolate seasons eventually come to an end: "Weeping may stay for the night, but rejoicing comes in the morning."

WEEK ONE   DAY FIVE

Personal Application

*E*ach week you will spend your fifth day of study reflecting on the material you covered in the previous four lessons. I encourage you to use this format for review and reflection. Ask God to provide insight that will enable you to apply all that you are learning to your everyday life.

Application from Day One

After the Israelites settled in the Promised Land, the "people served the LORD throughout the lifetime of Joshua" (Judges 2:7). According to Judges 2:10, what was different about the next generation of Israelites?

_____

It is imperative that followers of God share Scripture and communicate their personal experiences of God's faithfulness with their children and grandchildren if we want to influence the next generation's spiritual health and faith. In the lesson for Day One, you were encouraged to reflect on a personal experience when you were convinced God fought for you or provided for you in a tangible way. (See page 3 in your workbook.)

Use the prompts below to write a short summary of your experience.

What was your situation?

_____

_____

How did you pray? What obstacle did you ask God to move, or what need did you ask God to meet?

_____

_____

What happened, and how did you recognize the results as God's action or provision?

_____

_____

Look back at your list of people in the next generation with whom you have influence (page 3).

Prayerfully ask at least one person from that list if you can share your story. Then do so using the outline above. Be prepared to share your story-telling experience with your Bible study friends the next time you meet. If you are not doing this study with a group, call a friend and share your experience.

Application from Days Two through Four

As we reflect on the lessons from the week, I want to take this opportunity to clarify one of the key points from our lesson.

Please once again read Joshua 23:9–13, and note everything the Israelites were supposed to avoid when they settled in the Promised Land.

_____

_____

_____

God's instructions to avoid intermarrying and associating with the people of other nations were about the focus of the foreign nations' worship, not their race. God wanted His people's hearts. He wanted purity of worship, not sterilization of genetics. He wanted unity of heart, not uniformity of skin tone. He wanted unwavering devotion, not unchanging physical characteristics.

> He wanted unity of heart, not uniformity of skin tone.

Look again at Judges 2:10–13. What actions angered the Lord?

_____

Sadly, passages like we studied this week have erroneously been used by some to perpetuate and support racial prejudice. As we prepare to get into the heart of our study on the book of Ruth, let's first take time to examine what Scripture tells us about people of different racial descent. Read the passages below, and note what you learn about God's heart toward people of all races.

Deuteronomy 10:16–19: _____

_____

Acts 10:34–35: _____

_____

James 2:8–9: _____

Revelation 7:9–17: _____

_____

Take a moment to reflect on all that you just read and the notes you have written above. Now I want to challenge you to answer the following questions thoughtfully and prayerfully.

What prejudices toward people of different races did you grow up believing?

_____

_____

What experiences do you think perpetuated those stereotypes?

_____

_____

_____

What physical characteristics prompt you to have a negative first impression of another person?

_____

_____

_____

One day, as believers in Christ, we will gather before God's throne with fellow Christians from every nation, language, and people group. Our unity will be based on our love for the Lord and our common salvation through faith. Take a moment to prayerfully confess any preconceived ideas you have about people of other nationalities, negative feelings toward people with different physical characteristics from your own, or hatred you may feel toward another human being for whatever reason.

As you pray, look up each of the passages below and use them as a springboard for your prayers:

Psalm 139:1–14   1 Samuel 16:7   Psalm 139:23–24   1 John 1:9

To finish this week ask God to give you a renewed sense of openness to all that God wants to teach you through his Word about loving your neighbor and the sin of racism or prejudice against our fellow human beings. Life this side of our eternal home can be difficult and trying, but we can get a taste of the sweetness of heaven when we love all people and stand hand in hand with all our brothers and sisters in Christ.

How good and pleasant it is when God's people live together in unity!

It is as if the dew of Hermon were falling on Mount Zion.

For there the LORD bestows His blessing, even life forevermore. (Psalm 133:1, 3)

Week 2

Exemplifying Kindness

WEEK TWO | DAY ONE

Loyalty Returned

When Naomi heard in Moab that the Lord had come to the aid of his people by providing food for them, she and her daughters-in-law prepared to return home from there.

RUTH 1:6

When we last saw Naomi, Ruth, and Orpah, they were adapting to life in Moab without the support and protection of their late husbands. These widows' future seemed bleak. However, a glimmer of hope appeared on the western horizon. What important change occurred back in Naomi's homeland that prompted the women to begin preparing for a trip westward toward Judah (Ruth 1:6)?

_____

Please read Ruth 1:7–9.

I imagine as the three women set out toward Judah, Naomi reflected upon the trip she and her family had taken along that same road some ten years earlier when they traveled from Judah to Moab. Family road trips, even on foot in ancient times, create life-long memories. Weary parents and their children bicker over inconveniences and laugh amid the common discomforts experienced during long and exhausting days of travel. I imagine Naomi's heart must have longed to hear the laughter of her sons or to stare knowingly once again into the eyes of her husband. Perhaps her mind wandered back to the life she had left behind in Bethlehem, remembering the people and imagining the joyful reunions that awaited her return. However, somewhere along that ancient dusty road, Naomi's thoughts seem to have settled on the difficulties that might lie ahead for her daughters-in-law as Moabite women seeking to make a new life in Judah. Naomi had come to Moab as an Israelite a decade earlier. She was familiar with the struggles of adapting to a different culture—especially amid people who were at odds with one's homeland. What directive did Naomi give her daughters-in-law in verse 8?

Interestingly, the usual phrasing for returning to one's family was to return to the "home of your father," yet Naomi chose to use the expression *betem*, or "house of a mother."[10] The phrase occurs only a few times in Scripture. Let's read a couple of those passages to gain insight into Naomi's thoughts as she directed the women to return to Moab.

The expression "house of a mother" is also used in Genesis 24 when describing Rebekah's home after she returned to tell her parents about her encounter with Abraham's servant when he was in search of a wife for Isaac. If you are familiar with the story, you know Rebekah accepted the servant's invitation to become Isaac's wife.

Each time the expression "house of a mother" is used in Scripture, it is in a context involving love and marriage.[11] Naomi's choice of this specific phrase seems intentional and probably communicated her heartfelt desire for her daughters-in-law to find love and remarry once again. I also wonder whether Naomi wanted her beloved companions to remarry so they would be released from any responsibility for her care. After all, no loving mother (or in-law) wants to be a burden to her children.

In Ruth 1:8, what did Naomi pray the Lord would do for the young women, and what was her stated reason for this specific prayer?

The word *kindness* (or *kindly*) in verse 8 is translated from the Hebrew word *hesed*, which is usually expressed in the context of loyalty, devotion, and commitment. When the Bible talks of the kindness of God, the term is linked with God's loving commitment toward His covenant people. Naomi prayed God would bestow the same kindness on Ruth and Orpah that He would display toward His covenant people, because Orpah and Ruth had apparently been kind to Naomi and to her sons, perhaps during their time of grief after the death of Elimelek.

I'm touched by the apparent love and sincere affection these two women expressed for their mother-in-law. Even in the best of circumstances, in-law relationships can be complicated by differing perspectives, unmet expectations, misinterpreted motives, or communication style differences. The loving relationship between these women and their commitment toward one another serve as a lovely example of a beautiful in-law relationship. If your in-law relationships need some work, take a moment now to lift those relationships before God and ask Him to help you do your part to make your family connections more like Naomi's.

Naomi's prayer was an act of loyal devotion and commitment toward her daughters-in-law. The three women were trapped by adverse circumstances, but Naomi prayed God would express His covenant kindness toward her daughters-in-law by freeing them from their hopelessly widowed state. She knew the two young women still had time to find new husbands if they returned to Moab. She probably feared that if they returned with her to Judah, they would forever remain poor Moabite widows without any hope of marrying Israelite men.

Read Ruth 1:9–10. How did the young women respond to Naomi's kind but firm directive?

_____

Now read Ruth 1:11–13.

Naomi's mention of the young women marrying one of her future sons seems strange from our modern-day American perspective. However, Naomi probably had in mind an Israelite custom called the levirate marriage, which will prove to be important later in the story.

In ancient Israel, when an Israelite man died without heirs, his next of kin had a responsibility to marry his dead relative's widow. The firstborn son from that union would be given the deceased man's name and would eventually inherit the family land and any other inheritance that would have passed to the mother's deceased former husband. However, if an Israelite refused to fulfill his duty to his relative's widow, she could take the matter before the city elders. If the leaders were unable to convince him to marry the widow, a stigma would follow the unwilling man from that day forward.[12] The scenario is outlined in Deuteronomy 25:5–10. Please take a moment to read those passages and answer the following questions.

According to verse 9, what steps would the rejected widow take to persuade her unwilling relative to honor his responsibility to carry on his brother's family line?

_____

If he refused, how would the unwilling man's family line be labeled?

_____

In ancient times, "legal title [to land] was symbolically claimed by walking over land; transfer of title therefore entailed passing the sandal; and renunciation of title was symbolized by removal of the sandal. In this case, for refusing to build up the deceased [brother's] name, the brother's own family was stigmatized by its name."[13] There would be no brothers to rescue the wives of deceased Mahlon and Kilion, and no nephews to carry on their names. If Ruth and Orpah traveled to Judah, Naomi recognized they could be destined to remain unmarried and poor for the rest of the lives. Naomi's kindness toward her beloved daughters-in-law was evident as she urged them to return to Moab and prayed God's covenant kindness over them.

In Ruth 1:13, what did Naomi say the Lord had done to her?

_____

Naomi apparently felt God had turned against her—perhaps like a brother rejecting the responsibility to marry his dead brother's wife. As she stood urging Ruth and Orpah to return to Moab, I can't help but wonder if Naomi's bitter circumstances had prompted her to feel unloved and abandoned by God. Yet this tragically childless widow's bitterness was eclipsed by her loving prayers for God to bless her daughters-in-law with the same loyalty and kindness she probably felt God had withheld from her.

As we will see later in our study, the kindness and loyalty that Naomi so selflessly prayed would be granted to Ruth and Orpah was eventually returned to Naomi by Ruth and the Lord.

WEEK TWO | DAY TWO

Bittersweet Reunion

"Don't call me Naomi," she told them. "Call me Mara, because the Almighty has made my life very bitter."

RUTH 1:20

Naomi's bitter circumstances prompted her to feel abandoned and rejected by God Himself. When life gets particularly difficult, sometimes we feel as though God does not notice our pain or doesn't care about our suffering. But what does Psalm 34:18 tell us about our Lord?

_____

When the struggles of this life break your heart and crush your spirit, our Lord draws close to you. He is there, even when you cannot sense His presence or feel His love. Maybe you need to be reminded of that truth for yourself today. As Naomi wrestled with the bitterness stirring within her heart, she still lovingly urged her daughters-in-law to save themselves by returning to Moab where she prayed they would find better lives securely settled in the homes of new husbands.

> When the struggles of this life break your heart and crush your spirit, our Lord draws close to you.

Let's see what happened as she urged them to return to Moab. Read Ruth 1:11–15.

Interestingly, to whom did Orpah return (v. 15)?

1). _____ 2). _____

Orpah didn't just return to Moab, she went back to fully embrace the people and the numerous gods of the Moabite culture. This is the last mention of Orpah in Scripture. We are not told whether she found a new husband or eventually had children. But the deliberate mention of returning to the "gods" of the Moabites makes me wonder whether Orpah shared her mother-in-law's bitterness over the tragic circumstances that she and Naomi attributed to God's neglect and abandonment.

Tragedies can prompt even the most devoted God-followers to question His faithfulness. When God does not do what we expect Him to do, our limited perspectives often cause us to question His goodness, and if we are not careful, our anger can lead to deeply rooted bitterness. In the aftermath of a heartbreak, even those who remain committed to their faith can experience some confusion about why a good, all-powerful God allows tragedies to occur in the lives of those He loves.

Have you ever experienced a tragedy or loss that caused you to question the faithfulness and goodness of God? If so, share some of the thoughts with which you wrestled as you attempted to process your grief and disappointment.

_____

_____

_____

Before we move on with our lesson, I just want you to know that I am profoundly saddened by the loss and disappointment you experienced. My heart is heavy as I write this because I have wrestled with similar thoughts and feelings myself. I am deeply sorry for the pain you have experienced, the loss you have endured, or the disappointment you have encountered along your journey with God. But if you are doing this study with me today, I suspect that means you have come to the realization that there are events that occur in this life that we will never fully understand and circumstances that will never seem right from our limited perspective. I trust that in the most painful moments of wrestling with the whys of your circumstances, you have decided to set your mind and heart in the loving hands of the only One who sees beyond the limitations of this life to the eternal benefits that will somehow come from your suffering and pain. God alone knows all the heartache you have felt, the questions you have asked, and the pain you have experienced. He alone knows the depth of glory that awaits you in eternity. Hold tightly to Him. He loves you and is worthy of your trust.

Let's take a moment to remind ourselves of a few truths about God's faithfulness and goodness. Please read each passage below and prayerfully note keywords that most encourage you today.

Psalm 9:9–10: _____

Psalm 103:13–14: _____

Psalm 107:1–9: _____

Nehemiah 9:19–21 (Note how God treated His people as they wandered in the desert after He delivered them from Egypt): _____

The same God who faithfully led the Israelites through the wilderness is close to you during your dry desert seasons of trial as well. I do not have answers to all your questions, and I, too, struggle to make sense of the tragedies of this life. But this is what I do know: turning from devotion to the One who created life and overcame death is never the answer. Orpah's life in Moab is not conveyed to us in Scripture, but I can assure you she never found peace or joy devoting herself to lifeless and powerless gods. In contrast, let's see how Ruth responded to Naomi's directive to return to Moab.

Please read Ruth 1:15–18.

Ruth's words are some of the most beautiful in all of Scripture. She expressed the essence of commitment. As I write this, I am helping to plan my daughter's wedding. I cannot help but think of a bride speaking these words to her groom on their wedding day. Watching a young bride express that depth of commitment to her God-following husband would prompt this usually composed believer in Christ to ugly cry right there in front of everyone attending the wedding. Oh, I hope I do not do that at Brianna's wedding (how embarrassing!), but I suspect there is a good chance I will do just that (picture the monkey covering its eyes emoji right here).

When Naomi realized the depth of Ruth's commitment to her, she conceded, and the two widows traveled together back to Bethlehem. Let's see what happened as they arrived back in Naomi's hometown.

Please read Ruth 1:19–22.

How did the town react, and what did the women say as Naomi entered Bethlehem (v. 19)?

_____

_____

The whole town apparently knew Naomi and the women's words seem to imply that Naomi's appearance was markedly different from her previous days in Bethlehem. Grief and hardship take their toll on us spiritually and emotionally, but sometimes they even effect our physical appearance. Naomi and Ruth returned to Bethlehem at the beginning of the barley harvest, which was in March or April each year.[14] I imagine as Naomi and Ruth walked into Bethlehem that cool spring morning, the "stir" described in verse 19 was probably prompted by the dramatic change in Naomi's appearance. Grief affects every aspect of our lives, and Naomi had been burdened by its insurmountable weight for over a decade.

As the women of Bethlehem gathered around Naomi and called her by name, what name did she say she should be called instead and why (v. 20)?

The name Naomi means "sweetness," whereas Mara means "bitter."[15] For this previously married mother of two, the name that perhaps fittingly described her previous life in Bethlehem no longer felt appropriate. It is possible that hearing her name from the lips of her former friends prompted a flood of sweet memories to cause a cavernous ache in the depths of Naomi's stomach. "Call me Mara," she exclaimed. I imagine the women who had known Naomi best wisely said the least. Perhaps after a long embrace, the women of Bethlehem made a comfortable place for the women from Moab to rest. Maybe they prepared a fresh, warm meal and sat supportively near as Naomi and Ruth shared their heartrending story. It was a bittersweet reunion for this woman whose former life in Beth-lehem had been full of relationships and sweet memories. Her reality probably felt painfully empty and riddled with bitter regrets.

WEEK TWO DAY THREE

Gleaning Favor

May the LORD repay you for what you have done. May you be richly rewarded by the LORD, the God of Israel, under whose wings you have come to take refuge.

RUTH 2:12

As our previous lesson closed, Naomi and Ruth were safely back with friends in Bethlehem, relaying the series of tragic losses they had experienced during their time in Moab. It was a bittersweet reunion for the previously fruitful Naomi, who had left Bethlehem to escape a regional famine. Sadly, she returned to the once again harvest-ripe city with a famine of hope nestled deeply within her grief-laden heart.

According to Ruth 1:22, what was taking place in Bethlehem as the women arrived?

_____

According to Merrill Tenney, "barley was the main staple bread plant of the Hebrews and the main food for the poor."[16] The barren "House of Bread" Naomi had left over a decade earlier was now ripe with grain. Ruth knew she and Naomi needed food, and she was determined to glean some of that abundant crop.

Please read Ruth 2:1–3.

What did Ruth propose to do behind the harvesters? _____

The grain left behind during the harvest were called *gleanings.* According to Leviticus 23:22, what was their purpose?

_____

God provided for the poor, the foreigners, and the widows by commanding His people to leave a part of their abundance behind for those who were willing to do the tedious work of gathering the scraps left behind by the harvesters. Gleaning was the process of gathering those scraps.

Read Deuteronomy 24:19–22. What did God promise to do for those who left behind a portion of their harvest for the poor and needy (v. 19), and what past season of hardship was the focus of this command (v. 22)?

_____

The property owners' act of obedience served as a reminder to the Israelite people that God had provided for their ancestors when they had been oppressed and needy slaves in Egypt. Providing for the poor also reminded them that God faithfully brought the Israelites out of their poor and needy state in Egypt and graciously led them into the fruitful land they harvested.

Read each of the following passages, and note what you learn about God's provision for the poor as well as His response to those who share their abundance with people in need.

Deuteronomy 15:11: _____

Proverbs 14:21: _____

Proverbs 22:9: _____

According to 1 John 3:17–18, what prompts generosity toward people in need?

_____

God lovingly provided for widows like Naomi and Ruth through the obedience and open-handed generosity of the Israelites. In fact, He still provides for the poor and needy through the obedience and generosity of His people. Begin praying about how you can be more open handed and generous toward people around you who are struggling due to financial hardships or tragic circumstances. Ask God to show you how to love people better by giving more generously.

Look again at Ruth 2:1–3. Who owned the field where Ruth gleaned, and what was his connection with Naomi?

_____

Ruth went into a field and began gleaning behind the harvesters. Lo and behold, she ended up working in the field owned by a relative of Naomi's late husband, Elimelek. This is a good time to introduce another key concept of our study: God's providence.

> **God's providence:** His infinite ability to accomplish His divine purposes on earth as well as in our lives.

Our Lord is Creator of everything, and He is omniscient. He is able to orchestrate situations and events divinely to provide protective and spiritual care for His people. All creation is under God's sovereign control, and He knows past, present, and future. He is able to guide His people and control circumstances to accomplish His purposes. He can guide a needy widow to a field owned by her late husband's relative. God can inspire a wealthy landowner to take pity on a hardworking woman gleaning in his field. As we will see, God did exactly that.

> All creation is under God's sovereign control, and He knows past, present, and future.

Please read Ruth 2:4–7.

What do you learn about Ruth from these passages?

_____

What do you learn about Boaz from these passages?

_____

There is nothing I find more endearing than someone with a strong work ethic. Ruth appears to have possessed that trait. And other than church staff positions, I do not ever remember a boss greeting me or my coworkers with words like, "The Lord be with you!" (Did you notice the explanation point? How cool is that?) Boaz would be receiving his favorite muffin and coffee on Boss's Day from this staffer, for sure.

Now read Ruth 2:8–10.

How does Boaz address Ruth? _____

Interestingly, Boaz was probably closer in age to Naomi than Ruth. I imagine he spoke to Ruth with a fatherly tone as he encouraged her to remain safely in his field with the women who worked for him. Look again at verse 9. What did Boaz do to ensure Ruth would be safe while working in his field?

_____

How did Ruth respond to Boaz's kindness toward her (v. 10)?

_____

Now read Ruth 2:11–16.

Boaz ensured Ruth would be able to glean plenty of grain for herself and Naomi. He not only ordered his men to allow her to gather whatever scraps they left behind, but he told them to intentionally pull out entire stalks and leave them behind for her to pick up.

The Hebrew word translated "favor" (v. 10) usually refers to "beneficent treatment of another by one who is under no obligation to extend favor. Such favor is an expression of compassion"; the Hebrew term can also be translated as "kindness."[17] Ruth seems to have been overwhelmed and a bit bewildered by the kindness of this wealthy Israelite stranger. Look back at Ruth 2:2. What did Ruth seem to recognize she would require in order to glean in someone's field?

_____

Look at verses 11–12 again. What prompted Boaz's kindness toward Ruth?

_____

I suspect kindness was part of Boaz's character, but Ruth was experiencing the favor of the God she chose to follow, as well as the compassion of a man who had heard her tragic story. I would say Ruth was gleaning far more than grain in Boaz's field. Ruth was gleaning favor.

WEEK TWO DAY FOUR

A Man of Standing

Now Naomi had a relative on her husband's side, a man of standing from the clan of Elimelek, whose name was Boaz.

RUTH 2:1

Yesterday's lesson ended with Ruth gleaning favor as well as a substantial amount of grain under the protection of the hired workers in Boaz's field. Look at Ruth 2:1. How is Boaz described?

_____

Depending on the version, your Bible may describe Boaz as a "worthy man" (ESV), a "man of standing" (NIV), or maybe even "a man of great wealth and influence" (AMP). However he is described, Boaz was a man of influence in Bethlehem. Before we find out what happened next in Ruth's journey, let's attempt to understand more about this man named Boaz who will join Ruth at center stage for the remainder of our study.

The name Boaz means "strength" or "fleetness."[18] Interestingly, the left pillar of Solomon's temple was called Boaz because of its strength. I don't know whether Boaz's physique measured up to his name, but from the little that is recorded about Boaz in Scripture, he seems to have also possessed strength of character.

Read Ruth 2:1–16, and note any words or actions by Boaz that reflect strength of character.

_____

_____

_____

Boaz was from a long line of strong leaders, the most notable of whom were his grandfather and his mother.

Fill in the names of Boaz's line from 1 Chronicles 2.

Boaz's father was (v. 11) _____.

(Jewish tradition holds that Salmon was one of the two spies Joshua sent to Jericho to "look over the land" [Joshua 2:1].[19])

Boaz's grandfather was (v. 11) _____.

How is his grandfather described in verse 10? _____

Boaz's great-grandfather was (v. 10) _____.

Moses's brother Aaron, who was also the first high priest and father of the priestly line of Israel, married Amminadab's daughter, Elisheba. That makes Nahshon Aaron's brother-in-law.

A couple years after God brought His people out of Egypt, Moses was told to take a census of the men twenty years and older who could serve in Israel's army. A leader was chosen from each tribe to assist with the count. According to Numbers 1:5–7, what leader from the tribe of Judah was chosen for this important task?

_____

Later, when Moses completed the original tabernacle and dedicated it to the Lord, a leader from each of the twelve tribes of Israel brought offerings for the dedication of the tabernacle's altar.

Read Numbers 7:11–12, and note the first leader who brought the offering on behalf of his tribe: _____

In addition to a legacy of strong leaders on his father's side, Boaz's mother also had an important role in Israel's history. Read Matthew 1:4–5 and note the name of Boaz's mother. (Spoiler alert: verse 5 also reveals where Ruth's relationship with Boaz was going).

Boaz's mother was _____.

Let's read about the significance of Boaz's mother, Rahab, in Israel's first victory as they fought to secure their Promised Land.

Read all of Joshua 2, and answer the questions below:

What was Rahab's occupation in Jericho (v. 1)? _____

According to verses 4–6, what did Rahab do to protect the Israelite spies?

_____

Reread verses 8–11. What surprising statements did this Canaanite prostitute make as she spoke to the two Israelite spies?

_____

_____

_____

_____

According to verse 12, what did Rahab request be shown toward her family, and on what basis did she make this appeal?

_____

Kindness appears to have been a family tradition in Boaz's family. Read the following verses, and note what else you learn about Boaz's mother, Rahab.

According to Joshua 6:22–25, what relatives did Rahab save by protecting the spies?

_____

_____

According to Hebrews 11:31, what prompted Rahab's actions in Jericho?

_____

What do you learn about Rahab from James 2:25?

_____

Boaz's mother was a courageous woman who displayed great faith in the "God in heaven above and on earth below" (Joshua 2:11) and who "dried up the water of the Red Sea" (Joshua 2:10) when He freed His people from slavery. Rahab played an important role in the Israelites' conquest of the land of Canaan. Her actions helped God's people take possession of the very Promised Land where Boaz's fertile farm was located.

The landowner who greeted his employees with a joyful acknowledgement of God (Ruth 2:4) probably grew up watching his dad and grandfather lead other men in Judah. We don't know if he knew of his mom's sordid past, but I suspect, at a minimum, he knew the story of how Rahab hid his father and the other spy and helped bring about victory for the nation of Israel.

WEEK TWO   DAY FIVE

Personal Application

Application from Day One

To refresh your memory, reread Ruth 1:6–10. As Naomi urged Orpah and Ruth to return to Moab, what did she pray the Lord would do for her two beloved daughters-in-law?

_____

The Hebrew word for kindness is *hesed*. Look back at this week's Day One lesson on page 23, and reread the paragraph with an explanation of the word *hesed*. What is especially significant about God's expression of *hesed*?

_____

_____

Naomi prayed the Lord would treat Orpah and Ruth with the loyalty and loving devotion with which He would treat one of His committed and devoted people—with *hesed*, kindness. The Lord treats His people with merciful, gracious kindness, and His favor was

Naomi's heartfelt desire for Ruth and Orpah. In fact, I would say Naomi's prayerful desire for her daughters-in-law to find husbands was in itself an act of loving kindness.

According to Ephesians 4:32–5:2, how should the kindness and love God expresses toward us influence our behavior toward others?

_____

_____

Application from Day Two

Hesed is usually expressed in the context of devotion and commitment. I can think of no greater example of commitment from Scripture than Ruth's words to her mother-in-law, Naomi, when she refused to return to Moab.

Reread Ruth 1:16.

Let's turn some of Ruth's words to Naomi into a prayer of commitment to our God. Fill in the blanks below (from the NIV version of the Bible) and use it as a prayer prompt as you say it back to God.

Where you _____, I will _____, and where you _____ I will

_____. Your people will be my _____.

Our Lord has shown abundant kindness toward us. How can we not express loving kindness to His people? Our people. One way we express our love for God is by loving others.

Now read 1 John 4:7–17.

According to verse 17, how is love made complete among us?

_____

Love as Jesus loved (sacrificially). Be merciful as Jesus showed mercy (lavishly). Be gracious as Jesus imparted grace (consistently).

Reflect on the women in your sphere of influence. Can you name at least one woman you would say is loving, merciful, and gracious toward others and reflects Jesus to the world around her? Take a moment to thank God for her example and to pray that you, too, can be like Jesus to the people around you.

Dear friends, since God so loved us, we also ought to love one another. (1 John 4:11)

Application from Day Three

Look back at the focus passage at the top of this week's Day Three lesson. How is God's protection and favor described at the end of this verse?

_____

Read the following passages, and note what insight you gain into the meaning of this metaphor.

Deuteronomy 32:9–11: _____

_____

Psalm 91:1–4: _____

_____

Matthew 23:37: _____

When we take refuge under the protection and care of our Heavenly Father through faith in Jesus, His Son, we find the kindness and favor of God. He shields and protects us. He lovingly meets our needs. Even when He nudges us from our comfortable places of complacency or allows us to make mistakes so we learn and grow, His discipline is always for our good. Ruth chose to leave behind the false gods of her Moabite heritage to instead take refuge under the faithful and loving protection of the one true God. When we are afraid, we can rest in the fact that our Lord cares for us and watches over us much like a hen covers her chicks under her loving wings. When we are in need, we can find favor and rest under His watchful care.

> When we take refuge under the protection and care of our Heavenly Father through faith in Jesus, His Son, we find the kindness and favor of God.

What is your greatest need right now? How are you encouraged by the passages we read today and the truth that you can find favor and protection as a follower of our Lord?

_____

_____

_____

_____

Application from Day Four

In our Day Four lesson, we learned more about a faithful and generous man named Boaz. What character traits did "the man of standing" from Elimelek's family possess that were probably passed along to him by his older family members?

_____

_____

Rahab was once a prostitute, but because she took refuge under the wings of the God of "heaven above and the earth below," she became a vital part of Israel's faith story. How do you think Rahab's story might have influenced Boaz's kindness toward Ruth, a foreigner who chose to follow the God of Israel and become a part of their Bethlehem community?

_____

_____

Use the following prompts to write two sentences representing your faith story.

I once was _____.

I sought refuge in the Lord and now I am _____

_____.

Close this week's lesson by taking a moment to pray to the God of heaven above and earth below. Thank Him for His transformative work in your life. Be specific. Be thankful. He just may use your story to influence one of your descendants' faith story.

Week 3

A Weighty Proposal

The Weight of Generosity

So Ruth gleaned in the field until evening. Then she threshed the barley she had gathered, and it amounted to about an ephah. She carried it back to the town, and her mother-in-law saw how much she had gathered.

RUTH 2:17–18A

As our lessons closed last week, Boaz, the man of standing whose ancestors had a track record of leadership, faithfulness, and courage, had extended generosity and kindness to Ruth by allowing her to safely glean behind his hired harvesters.

Read Ruth's words to Boaz below from Ruth 2:13: "May I continue to find favor in your eyes, my lord," she said. "You have put me at ease by speaking kindly to your servant— though I do not have the *standing of one of your servants*" (emphasis added).

The Hebrew word translated as "servants" here in verse 13 is *sipha*. Its meaning gives us great insight into Ruth's view of herself. *Sipha* is a female servant of lowest rank. By claiming the status of *sipha*, Ruth was acknowledging that she had a status lower than the lowest of servants in the field, whereas Boaz was a man of high social standing.[20]

I remember feeling that way one time while attending a corporate holiday party at a swanky hotel located in an upscale area of downtown Houston. My husband, Mark, worked for a large oil company at the time. Most of the women at the party looked as though they had spent the day at a spa, preparing for the event. They had updos and fresh pedicures. They wore cocktail dresses adorned with what appeared to be expensive jewelry. I had spent the day running errands and playing with our kids. My nails were unpolished and short. The only jewelry I wore was my wedding ring and some inexpensive fashion earrings. I felt awkward, inadequate, and frumpy. I remember smiling at one of the servers carrying a tray as she backed through the black swinging doors that led to the kitchen. I kept thinking I probably had more in common with the women on the other side of those swinging doors than the women dining at our table. I pasted a smile on my face and did my best to join in with the small talk. Let's just say, I was glad when the evening was finally over.

When was the last time you were in a situation that made you feel inferior to the people with whom you were associating?

From what you know about Ruth so far, what circumstances might have magnified Ruth's sense of unworthiness as Boaz graciously extended her favor and kindness?

Boaz's generosity continued. Reread Ruth 2:13–16.

Now read Micah 7:1, and note what the verse implies about the plight of one who relied on gleaning for their food.

Gleaners typically gathered the leftovers of fruit and grain harvests. My grandmother would probably have said it was "slim pickins." Yet Boaz offered Ruth more roasted grain from his own table than she could eat. And when she finally went back out to glean in the field, Boaz instructed his men to pull out entire stalks from their bundles for her to easily pick up.

Look closely at Boaz's instructions to his men in Ruth 2:16. From where did the workers pull the stalks they left behind for Ruth?

Did you catch that? The men pulled harvested stalks from their bundles. Gleaners usually had to cut the leftover stalks themselves. Harvesting grain was difficult, tedious work. Yet all Ruth had to do was scoop up those loose stalks. Now, I am not suggesting Ruth was a taking it easy or didn't work hard that day in the fields. Look again at Ruth 2:7 and then verse 17. How long did Ruth work in the fields, and what did she do with the barley she gathered before returning home for the evening?

Not only was gleaning barley monotonous, exhausting work, but threshing was physical work as well. Threshing was done on what was called a *threshing floor*, which "could be any hard, compacted surface" made of rock or earth.[21] After working all day in the fields, Ruth would have beat the grain with what was called a *flail*—a long, flexible stick that separated the grain from the straw. Then the grain was piled into the center of the threshing floor, where Ruth would have winnowed the grain by using a fork and throwing it into the air. The physically taxing process further purified the grain through a process of sifting.[22] Ruth worked hard all day, but the amount of grain and provision she received far exceeded any amount normally expected for a poor gleaner gathering leftovers from the edges of a farmer's field.

Read Ruth 2:17–19.

According to verse 17, how much barley resulted from Ruth's gleaning?

Depending on which standard is used, an ephah of barley would have weighed between thirty and fifty pounds.[23] So after gleaning in the fields from morning to evening, threshing, and winnowing, Ruth headed toward town with about fifty pounds of barley as well as her leftovers from Boaz's dinner table. An ephah of barley was probably enough to feed the two widows for a couple weeks.

According to verse 19, how did Naomi respond?

I am going to take some liberty with the text and assume the questions and statement Naomi fired off, seemingly without so much as a pause, were said with wide-eyed amazement at the haul of grain Ruth brought back from the fields. And to top it off, Ruth brought Naomi a carry-out dinner from her leftover roasted grain. Ancient Judah didn't have fast-food restaurants or food delivery services. I'm going to guess that dinner-to-go was an uncommon occurrence for Naomi and Ruth.

Now read Ruth 2:20–23, and answer the following questions.

To whom did Naomi say Boaz showed kindness (v. 20)?

Naomi described Boaz as a close relative as well as what?

How long did Ruth continue to glean in Boaz's fields?

When Naomi saw the surprisingly generous gleaning of grain, she seemed to guess that Boaz was not only intentionally providing for two tragically poor widows in need of food, but was honoring her late husband, Elimelek, by caring for the needs of Naomi and Ruth. The barley and wheat harvest seasons would have lasted from late April to early June.[24] I wonder how many more takeout meals Ruth brought home to Naomi during that time? I suspect Boaz continued to show generosity and kindness as he allowed Ruth to safely glean extraordinary amounts of grain from his fields. I would also guess Ruth acquired some impressive upper-body strength as she regularly carried the weight of Boaz's generosity home to Naomi.

We will stop her for today. Rest up; we have some deep concepts to study this week. You may need an extra cup of coffee or two. I'll join you for that extra cup.

WEEK THREE   DAY TWO

Character Amid Hard Times

Boaz replied, "I've been told all about what you have done for your mother-in-law since the death of your husband—how you left your father and mother and your homeland and came to live with a people you did not know before."

RUTH 2:11

*I*n our previous lesson, Ruth worked all day in the field of her dead father-in-law's relative. The gentle, kind "man of standing" from Bethlehem had taken notice of her, protected her, and provided for her. His care revealed a depth of character that endeared this reader to him. But Boaz wasn't the only one who displayed tremendous depth of character in this story.

Ruth came to Bethlehem knowing only her mother-in-law. She had no girlfriends to talk to when she was feeling down. She couldn't have tea with a sister when she needed a break from the daily grinding of flour or gleaning in the field. To make things worse, Ruth was a Moabite—a nation that had been longtime adversaries of the people with whom she now lived. Ruth could have been bitter. She could have sunk into a state of paralyzing depression. However, Ruth did the exact opposite, and the people in Bethlehem noticed.

Let's peek ahead for a moment. How is Ruth described in Ruth 3:11?

_____

Proverbs 31 contains a well-known passage describing a "wife of noble character." Obviously, at this time, Ruth was not a wife, and all the scenarios described in Proverbs 31 do not apply to her. However, read Proverbs 31:10–31 and note the passages and phrases that do describe Ruth's actions after settling in Bethlehem. (I did two for you.)

Verse 14: She is like the merchant ships, bringing her food from afar.

Verse 15: She provides food for her family.

Verse _____

Verse _____

Verse _____

Read the following passages, and note the character traits they reveal:

Ruth 1:15–17: _____

Ruth 2:7, 11, 17: _____

Summarize the phrases and qualities you have listed above into one sentence that could be used to describe Ruth:

_____

When Ruth married Mahlon, she probably had all the dreams we women typically dream when we say our wedding vows. Perhaps she pictured several little Mahlons or Ruths running through her home. Maybe she and her groom made grand plans to return to Bethlehem and build a life together on the family land. Ruth had probably never even considered the possibility that she might end up a lonely widow without resources in her husband's homeland. Her circumstances thrust her into a state of hardship that could have rendered her bitter. Yet the hard times in Moab and Bethlehem revealed courage and a depth of honorable character we all can aspire to as we follow God and seek to honor Him, regardless of our circumstances.

Ruth's faithfulness and strength despite her hardships remind me of some passages from the book of Habakkuk. As we discussed earlier in our study, the Jews had a long history of seasons of rebellion against God. Habakkuk was a prophet, and the Lord revealed to him that God's judgment was forthcoming. In fact, the Lord told Habakkuk the Babylonians would oppress the people of Judah and God's people would endure great hardship for a season. However, God also assured Habakkuk that the season of scarcity and hardship would eventually come to an end. Habakkuk wrote a psalm of sorts, committing to trust in God's deliverance throughout the hardships. Read Habakkuk's psalm recorded in Habakkuk 3, then focus on verses 15–19.

Do verses 17–18 remind you of any period in your own journey through life? If so, briefly describe the situation:

_____

_____

_____

Why do you think Habakkuk was confident he would be able to rejoice in the Lord during the season of oppression and hardship?

_____

_____

Habakkuk knew God was faithful and He would eventually bring relief, just as He said He would. Habakkuk was also aware that the season of hardship had a purpose. Isn't that what we need to know when we are in a period of intense trial or spiritual drought? We need to know God hasn't forsaken us and He is using our hardship for some good in our hearts and some greater purpose. The truths of God's character and faithfulness sometimes elude us as we deal with daily struggles amid hard times. Yet Habakkuk's psalm stands as an encouraging example of trust in God during times of struggle and hardship. The book of Habakkuk assures us God was at work amid the Jews' hardships under Babylonian oppression. He had a plan, and He had a purpose. Those barren fig trees, empty vines, failed olive crops, and empty cattle stalls were all intended to deepen their hunger for their Lord and draw them back to Him.

> The truths of God's character and faithfulness sometimes elude us as we deal with daily struggles amid hard times.

As we will see in the coming weeks, God was at work in Ruth and Naomi's story too. It wasn't by chance that Ruth worked in Boaz's field. The women of Bethlehem noticed Ruth's loyalty and commitment to their old friend as well as to their God. Boaz recognized Ruth's work ethic and admired her steadfast character through all her heartrending tragedy and loss. God was right there working and providing for Ruth and Naomi, even when they didn't recognize it.

WEEK THREE

Read the following passages, and note the promises they hold.

Deuteronomy 31:8: _____

Psalm 34:18: _____

Matthew 11:28–29: _____

2 Corinthians 12:9–10: _____

James 1:2–4: _____

When times are tough, our discouragement can skew our perspective, but here's the truth: God is at work in your circumstances too. If you are in a barren season, trust that God is somehow using your lack to draw you closer to Him. If you are experiencing a series of trials (they seem to come in sets of three, don't they?), remember that the testing of your faith produces perseverance (James 1:3). If you are enduring unspeakable loss, draw strength from the truth that God is close to the brokenhearted. If you are worn out, Jesus graciously offers rest.

Ruth's reputation in her town as a woman of noble character was probably the result of steady, consistent, faithful choices she made that honored those she loved and glorified the God she chose to follow.

To close today's lesson, spend some time reflecting on the passages we studied today. Ask God to help you trust Him more deeply in times of hardship. Ask Him to strengthen you through your struggles such that others are inspired by your steadfast character amid hard times.

WEEK THREE | DAY THREE

A Thoughtful Plan

"I will do whatever you say," Ruth answered.

RUTH 3:5

Ruth's steadfast character amid her troubled and difficult times endeared the towns-people to her. Naomi benefited from Ruth's faithfulness. Ruth's tenacity intrigued Boaz. I would venture to say Ruth's daily schedule was probably exhausting, but she and Naomi were surviving, possibly even thriving in Bethlehem. However, concern for Ruth's future appears to have continued to weigh heavily on her mother-in-law's heart.

Reread Ruth 1:8–9. What two specific requests did Naomi make of the Lord as she prayed for her daughters-in-law?

1). _____

2). _____

I suspect Naomi continued to pray those prayers for Ruth (and maybe even for Orpah) and she was reflecting on those requests as we begin chapter 3 in the book of Ruth.

Read Ruth 3:1–5.

Recap Naomi's instructions to Ruth in your own words.

_____

_____

_____

_____

Now, there appears to have been some chemistry and romantic interest budding between Boaz and Ruth. Look back at Boaz's comment when he first laid eyes on Ruth gleaning in the field (Ruth 2:5). What was Boaz's question to the overseer of his harvesters?

In other words, is this woman taken? Is she married? We don't know the extent of Boaz's interest, but Ruth apparently caught this eligible older man's interest from the moment he saw her working in the field.

Look back at Boaz's response to Ruth (Ruth 2:8). What term of endearment did use with her?

Boaz was probably quite a bit older than Ruth, but he may have been quite smitten with her. We don't know what details from her conversations with Boaz that Ruth shared with Naomi, but his kindness and protective care over her were evident by that fifty-pound haul of grain she brought home the first night after working in Boaz's field, not to mention his continued provision for her throughout the barley and wheat harvests (Ruth 2:23).

Naomi appears to have been paying attention to the chemistry between Boaz and Ruth. What did Naomi say to Ruth in Ruth 3:1?

Interestingly, the phrase "find a home" in the New International Version of this passage is translated from a single Hebrew word that Naomi also used in her prayer back in Ruth 1:9, translated as "find rest." The word conveys "the security that comes from marriage" as well as relief from a life of poverty and possible exploitation.[25] Naomi loved Ruth and affectionately called her "daughter," just as Boaz had done. This mother-in-law's heartfelt prayer had apparently remained the same since that day on the road between Moab and Bethlehem when she urged both Ruth and Orpah to return to their mothers' homes in Moab—Lord, "grant [Ruth] rest in the home of another husband."

I wonder if Naomi had been asking God whether Ruth's seemingly coincidental work in the field of Elimelek's relative Boaz was His doing. She had been praying. Was this her answer? As our story continues, we will discover the answer to that question is a solid yes. And because Naomi had been diligently praying for Ruth, she recognized God's presence at work in the details.

Can you think of a time when you were diligently praying, possibly even crying out to God (on someone else's behalf or maybe even for yourself), and because you were watching and seeking God's answer, you recognized His active presence at work in your circumstances? If so, describe the circumstances below. If you can't recall a time when that happened, use the lines below to pray for God to enable you to recognize His activity around you, working on your behalf.

_____

_____

_____

_____

Naomi had been praying, and it appears she also had been watching for God to answer her prayers. She recognized God at work in the details of their circumstances. Ruth simply intended to glean barley and gather some food. God's providence was evident as she ended up working in the very field owned by Elimelek's relative (Ruth 2:3). Not only that, but Boaz had heard about Ruth's faithfulness to Naomi and how she had left her homeland to become a part of the Jewish community in Bethlehem (Ruth 2:11). It was no coincidence that Boaz was one of their "guardian-redeemers" (Ruth 2:20). And to further solidify God's presence in this seemingly chance meeting, Boaz appeared to have a romantic interest in Ruth.

That is how God works. We pray and seek Him and do our best to follow Him. We go about our everyday lives, working, serving, and trusting Him to meet our needs and guide our paths. We shouldn't be surprised when God orchestrates details to accomplish His purposes and meet our needs.

According to John 5:17, how often is God working? _____

Naomi recognized God at work. I can imagine this matchmaking mother-in-law's thoughts: *Ruth's gleaning in Boaz's field is no coincidence. This is God at work. This is His answer to my prayer for her to find security in the home of another husband. I don't want Ruth to mess this up. I had better give her some guidance.*

Now, I had to chuckle as I read Naomi's detailed instructions to Ruth. Ruth strikes me as a no-frills kind of woman.

> We shouldn't be surprised when God orchestrates details to accomplish His purposes and meet our needs.

She probably didn't focus a lot of attention on her appearance. After all, she had all that barley and wheat to glean. Maybe Naomi was afraid Ruth would go straight from the harvesting field to the threshing floor without thinking twice about her appearance. I can hear her saying, "Don't go to the threshing floor in your smelly work clothes, Ruth. You want to look and smell your best." Whatever the scenario, Naomi felt compelled to give Ruth some detailed instructions regarding the proper way to secure Boaz's affections.

What were Naomi's exact instructions to Ruth regarding her appearance in verse 3?

_____

_____

Naomi had a well thought-through plan. She told Ruth what to wear and even gave instructions about the timing of her encounter with Boaz. She did not want Ruth to approach him when he was distracted by work or while he was enjoying the evening meal. Naomi may have thought she was controlling the details of this encounter, but God was at work carrying out His divinely orchestrated plan. Naomi was simply a participant.

Ruth assured Naomi she would carefully execute the plan and headed out to the threshing floor. In tomorrow's lesson, we will see how Naomi's carefully crafted plan played out. But for today, reflect on the evidence of God's providential care in Ruth's life and in your own circumstances today. Bask in the knowledge that our God is infinitely able to accomplish His purposes for Ruth and for you.

WEEK THREE | DAY FOUR

Seeking Coverage

"Who are you?" he asked. "I am your servant Ruth," she said. "Spread the corner of your garment over me, since you are a guardian-redeemer of our family."

RUTH 3:9

Naomi's plan had been carefully discussed, and Ruth was dressed in her threshing-floor best. I imagine she carefully made her way through the crowds to an obscure, quiet spot where she could see Boaz yet remain unnoticed. As I think of Ruth watching and waiting, I find myself wondering if the scent of her carefully applied perfume served as an aromatic reminder that her and Naomi's survival might very well hinge on Boaz's response to this bold proposal. Let's see how Ruth implemented Naomi's detailed and possibly life-altering plan.

To begin, refresh your memory by reading Ruth 3:1–7.

Winnowing was done in the evening when strong breezes would carry the chaff away from the good, nourishing grain.[26] We don't know how long Ruth secretly watched Boaz winnow barley before he finally finished his work and headed to eat his evening meal. However long it took, Ruth patiently waited, just as she had been instructed. I imagine her heart pounded wildly in her chest as Boaz finished the last few bites of his food, wiped the crumbs from his beard, and slowly slid away from the table. Did she rehearse what she would say to Boaz? Did her palms sweat as she watched him walk to the far end of the grain pile and settle in for the night? We don't know what Ruth was thinking as she sat silently in her position nearby. But as the men found their places on the threshing floor for the night and the bustle of daily activity ceased, Ruth waited until the "man of standing," who had been so kind to her throughout the barley and wheat harvests, fell asleep. At the right time, Ruth probably took a deep breath, said a prayer, and quietly made her way to the end of the grain pile where Boaz was sleeping. What did Ruth do once she made it to Boaz (v. 7)?

As Naomi hatched this plan, she placed tremendous faith in God's ability to bring about His desired outcome. Ruth's actions there on the threshing floor were not your everyday actions of a virtuous women in Bethlehem. At harvest time, men often spent the night on the threshing floor to guard their valuable grain from thieves or wild animals.[27] It was common for prostitutes to go out to the threshing floor and offer their services.[28] Boaz could have misinterpreted Ruth's actions that night as a sexual proposition. After all, as a Moabite, Ruth's heritage was probably riddled with perversion. Yet Ruth carefully carried out the plan exactly as Naomi had instructed. Or did she? What did Naomi say would happen after Ruth uncovered Boaz's feet (v. 4)?

Hmm. Let's see what actually happened. Read Ruth 3:8–9. Who told whom what to do next (v. 9)?

I smiled as I compared Ruth's actions with Naomi's instructions. Maybe Ruth was a little concerned her actions would be misinterpreted. Rather than waiting for Boaz to tell her what to do, Ruth quickly made her intentions clear. What did Ruth ask Boaz to do (v. 9)?

I found Ruth's request puzzling. But after some research, I discovered that her words are gloriously important to the overarching message of our study. The phrase "corner of your garment" in the NIV is translated from a single Hebrew word *kanaph*, which is sometimes translated as "wings" and other times translated as "corner or edge of a garment or robe," depending on the version of the Bible. Let's explore the meaning of the word *kanaph* together. Each of the passages below contains the word *kanaph*. Read them, note how the word is translated, and then note the basic context in which *kanaph* is used. I have filled in the first one for you.

Verse	English Word	Context
Ezekiel 16:8	garment	The Lord compared Jerusalem to a naked young woman over whom He spread the corner of His garment.
Ruth 2:12		
Ruth 3:9		
Psalm 17:1, 8		
2 Chronicles 5:7–8		

I researched the men's outer garments in an effort to fully understand why the corners were called "wings," and I came across some information in *Illustrated Manners and Customs of the Bible*: "The Hebrew men wore an 'outer garment' consisting of a square or oblong cloth 2 to 3 m (80 to 120 in.) wide. This garment was called the coat, robe, or mantle. It was wrapped around the body as a protective covering with two corners of material in the front."[29]

These corners in the front of the garments were called wings, probably because they would look a bit like wings when they blew in the wind. Ruth 2:12 translates *kanaph* as "wings," and according to *The Bible Knowledge Word Study*, "the metaphor is that of a baby bird finding shelter under its mother's protective wings."[30] Like the outer garment, a mother bird would cover her babies with her wings. Ruth had chosen to leave behind Moab and all the idols of that culture to remain with Naomi for the rest of her days (Ruth 1:17), but she also took refuge under the authority and protection of Naomi's God.

> These corners in the front of the garments were called wings . . .

55

> **Refuge:** A shelter or protection from danger or distress, a place that provides that shelter or protection, or something to which one has recourse in difficulty.[31] A refuge offers security, provision, mercy, and peace.

In Psalm 46, the psalmist sings of what it means when God is our refuge. Psalm 23 conveys the shepherding love our Lord provides to those who take refuge in Him. Thoughtfully read these two psalms, and note phrases that convey the security, provision, mercy, and peace we find when God is our refuge.

_____

_____

_____

_____

As Ruth's story of redemption unfolds, she does indeed experience God as her refuge. Boaz was simply the vessel God used to accomplish His plan and purposes. How did Naomi describe Boaz in Ruth 2:20?

_____

A guardian-redeemer could buy back a family member from slavery, buy back property a family member had been forced to sell, and was responsible for raising offspring for a deceased relative.[32] As we close, how did Ruth refer to Boaz in Ruth 3:9?

_____

Ruth called on Boaz to step up and take his place as her guardian-redeemer. She asked him to cover her, not simply with the corner of his garment to shelter her from the elements that night on the threshing floor, but this woman of noble character who was willing to risk her reputation and her dignity to find refuge for herself and her beloved mother-in-law asked to be covered under the _kanaph_ of her redeemer—who was ultimately the Lord Himself.

Personal Application

"Who are you?" he asked. "I am your servant Ruth," she said. "Spread the corner of your garment over me, since you are a guardian-redeemer of our family."

RUTH 3:9

*T*oday, we will deviate from our usual Day Five format to focus on general information that helps us apply to our lives what we are learning.

Ruth sought shelter under Boaz's *kanaph*, but ultimately, she sought refuge under the *kanaph* of the God of Israel (Ruth 2:12). The God of Israel has identified Himself in Scripture using many names. Each name revealed an expression of His character and power applied to the situation in which His people found themselves, and each name was revealed as a means of helping His people understand that He was exactly what they needed in their specific situation. In fact, He is exactly what we need in any situation. There is a name for God I want to focus on as our personal application emphasis this week.

Look at Boaz's words to Ruth in Ruth 2:12:

*May the **LORD** repay you for what you have done. May you be richly rewarded by the **LORD**, the God of Israel, under whose wings you have come to take refuge"* (emphasis added).

Whenever you see the word LORD in all capital letters in Scripture, the name of God being expressed is Yahweh. It is also translated as I AM. The first time God revealed Himself by this name was when Moses was before God at the burning bush. God commissioned him to rescue the people of Israel from slavery in Egypt. Moses was gripped with fear. He felt completely inadequate. He couldn't even believe God would assign such a task to someone like him.

Take a moment to read God's words to Moses in Exodus 3:13–15 for yourself. Note your thoughts below:

_____

_____

God's name *Yahweh* conveys His active presence in our lives today. He was Yahweh in Moses's day—the God who was active and able to redeem His people from slavery in Egypt. He was Yahweh in Ruth and Boaz's day—the God who was active and able to richly reward Ruth for her faithfulness by allowing her to take refuge under the protection of His *kanaph*. Yahweh is active and present in the todays of the past, the todays of our lives now, and the todays of the future. He is the I AM. As He told Moses, God's active presence is with you, and He is actively working on your behalf in the present. All the time.

What does the fact that God is continually and actively present in your current circumstances mean to you right now?

_____

_____

As Ruth sought refuge under the *kanaph* of Yahweh, she was in need of a guardian-redeemer. There were no sons to come from Naomi to carry on Mahlon's name. There was no brother-in-law to marry Ruth and provide the protection and care she and Naomi desperately needed. Ruth sought out Boaz and asked him to cover her with his *kanaph*, but Ruth's hope rested solely in *Yahweh*, who, by the way, is also the ultimate Redeemer.

Look up each of the following verses, and note what other significant name is paired with LORD (Yahweh):

Psalm 19:14: _____

Isaiah 41:13–14: _____

Isaiah 43:14–15: _____

The God of Israel is *Yahweh*, the actively present Redeemer of His people. He is God the Father, Creator and King of all mankind. He is Ruth's Redeemer, and He is our Redeemer.

The *New International Encyclopedia of Bible Words* explains what is called "the language of redemption" this way: "The language of redemption often placed God in the role of

WEEK THREE

Israel's near kinsman, who acted to deliver His people from danger. Redemption from Egypt was not only an act of purchase but also the action of a kinsman moved by love."[33]

A guardian-redeemer, sometimes translated as "kinsman-redeemer," was a close relative who could buy back family members who had been sold into slavery or buy back a relative's property that had been sold under hardship (Leviticus 25:25). The kinsman-redeemer was also charged with the responsibility of marrying his deceased relative's widow in order to produce an heir and carry on the family line (Deuteronomy 25:5–10).

A kinsman-redeemer was a family member who was able to redeem what had been lost, whether personal freedom, a family's property, or the continuation of a family name. But the relative had to be willing and able to pay the redemption price.

Yahweh is the Redeemer. According to Hebrews 1:3, how did God reveal Himself to the world?

_____

According to Hebrews 2:9–11, what is Jesus's relationship to each of us as those who have been made holy through faith in Him?

_____

What does Romans 6:23 indicate is the punishment for sin? _____

Now read 1 Timothy 2:5–6. What did Jesus do for all people?

_____

And finally, write John 3:16 below:

_____

_____

Jesus is God the Son who is "the radiance of God's glory and the exact representation of His being" (Hebrews 1:3). He came to earth and suffered death, taking the penalty we deserved for our sin upon Himself. Jesus is our brother. He is our Kinsman-Redeemer. Jesus willingly suffered death on the cross in order to pay the redemption price for our sins. You have been purchased. You have been redeemed.

> Jesus willingly suffered death on the cross in order to pay the redemption price for our sins.

Jesus died for the sins of all people for all time, and anyone who believes He is who He says He is will no longer perish but will live for eternity as brothers and sisters with our LORD, Yahweh, our Redeemer, who revealed Himself to the world through the person of Jesus Christ.

Look up one final passage today. Write Ephesians 1:7 below, and rejoice in the assurance we have through Christ:

_____

_____

_____

We can take refuge under Yahweh's *kanaph* because our Kinsman-Redeemer shed His blood on our behalf. Next week we will discover more of what Scripture tells us about the benefits of finding refuge in God's redeeming love. For today, rejoice because our Kinsman-Redeemer died to redeem what was lost. That is you, beloved. I would say that is worth celebrating.

Week 4

Defining Refuge

Refuge Means Security

God is our refuge and strength, an ever-present help in trouble.

PSALM 46.1

When we last saw Ruth, she was sitting at Boaz's feet on the town's fleshing floor, boldly asking him to cover her with his *kanaph* and to act as her guardian-redeemer. Ultimately, Ruth sought the refuge of Yahweh, the powerful, actively present God of Israel who still offers refuge to anyone who seeks Him today by placing their faith in Jesus, the Redeemer of all humankind.

Look back at the definition of *refuge* on page 56 of your workbook, and write the three definitions below:

1). _____

2). _____

3). _____

Before we move forward with the story of Naomi, Ruth, and Boaz, this week I want to spend our study time exploring what it means for us to take refuge under Yahweh's *kanaph* by placing our faith in Jesus.

How did the Lord describe Himself in Isaiah 41:14?

_____

How is Jesus described in Hebrews 1:3?

_____

At Jesus's baptism, God spoke from heaven. How did God explain his relationship with Jesus in Matthew 3:17?

_____

When we choose to take refuge under the protection and security of God the Father through faith in God the Son, we receive security, provision, mercy, and peace. Today I want to focus on the security we have as believers in Jesus. God the Redeemer (Isaiah 41:14) revealed Himself through Jesus, who is God the Son (Matthew 3:17), the radiance of God's glory and the exact representation of His being (Hebrews 1:3a). When we associate ourselves with Him by faith, He covers us with His *kanaph* and we find refuge under His loving protection.

Look back at Psalm 46:01. How is the Lord described?

_____

An ever-present help means just that. The fancy term we use to describe this ever-present nature of God is *omnipresent*.

God's omnipresence: God is present everywhere, all the time, at the same time.

Reflect on God's omnipresence for a moment. It's mind blowing, isn't it? We humans are limited by space and time, but God is not. He is everywhere, all the time, at the same time. He sees everything we do. He hears everything we say (that's intimidating!). He is everywhere in our world. But I want you to grasp the truth that He is with you in *your* world—your everyday, take-care-of-the-house-and-the-kids-(or grandkids)-and-go-to-work world. He is with you as you swing wearily by the grocery store on the way home. He is with you as you scramble to throw a load of laundry into the wash and get to an appointment on time. He is with you when you care for your elderly parent and don't know what all the needs are, let alone how you will possibly meet them. Yahweh is with you when you are in pain, and He is with you when you are healthy. He is with you all the time. He is omnipresent. Whatever your circumstances, our Lord is an ever-present source of help for you. That, beloved, means security.

> Whatever your circumstances, our Lord is an ever-present source of help for you.

Look up the passages below, and note what they teach you about God's presence with you:

Psalm 23: _____

Isaiah 41:10: _____

Zephaniah 3:17: _____

Because God is with us all the time, we are never alone. How does that truth encourage you as you reflect on your circumstances today?

_____

_____

_____

Taking refuge in Christ means He is always with you. He is your Shepherd, and He cares for you. But the greatest security you have through faith in Christ is your eternal salvation.

Read John 3:16–18. Who has eternal life? _____

Would you be able to explain what it means to believe in Jesus (John 3:16) to someone who has never been introduced to the concept? Let's take a few minutes to solidify the concept such that we can write out a concise, simple explanation.

Before you begin, reflect on each of the following passages. Use a version of Scripture with which you are comfortable and that is easy for you to understand. Make notes here in the margin or on another piece of paper to help you collect your thoughts. Take a moment to pray and ask your ever-present Lord for help as you begin.

Romans 3:20–24   Romans 6:19–23   Romans 5:6–8   Romans 10:9–13

On the lines below, write your simple explanation of what it means to believe in Jesus. (If you are doing this study with a group, be ready to share your answer with your Bible study friends.)

_____

_____

_____

_____

The greatest security we gain through faith in Jesus is the gift of eternal life (Romans 6:23). I must ask you this question as we close today: Have you found refuge in Jesus? Have you asked Him to forgive your sins? Do you believe He is the Son of God who came to earth to die for your sins? Have you professed your faith (Romans 10:9)? The conclusions you reach about Jesus's identity and how you choose to respond to Him are the most important decisions you can make during your time on this earth.

If you have not made a profession of faith in Jesus, talk with your Bible study leader today and ask questions until you understand who Jesus is and are ready to accept the free gift of salvation He offers.

Finding refuge in God's redeeming love means you have the Lord with you through every challenge and every victory you experience during your life. You never walk alone. But the greatest security you have when you place your faith in Jesus is everlasting life in His presence.

To close today, read Revelation 21:1–5.

We will live for eternity with our Lord. We will be His people, and He will be our God (v. 3). He loves you so much that He sent Jesus to die so you could find refuge in Him. One day, He will make all things new and you will be with Him forever. These words are trustworthy and true (v. 5).

That is security.

WEEK FOUR | DAY TWO

Refuge Means Provision

There is a river whose streams make glad the city of God, the holy place where the Most High dwells.

PSALM 46:4

Yesterday we focused on the security we have when we find refuge under God's *kanaph* through faith in Jesus. Today, I want to focus on another aspect of God's providential care for us. When we find refuge in Jesus, we can count on our Redeemer and ever-present Helper to provide for us.

Now, I want to be clear that I am in no way suggesting life this side of our heavenly eternal home will be easy. I am not saying we are entitled to a fancy house, plenty of money in our bank accounts, gourmet meals, or closets full of clothing. In fact, God's Word does not promise any of those things. So let's start today by solidifying some of our theology when it comes to the provision of God.

Read 1 Timothy 6:3–19, and note the warnings and insight they contain regarding our attitudes toward possessions and wealth. Be sure to list verses in parentheses so you can discuss your findings with your Bible study friends.

Truths: _____

_____

_____

_____

Warnings: _____

_____

_____

_____

Now read the apostle Paul's words to the Philippians in Philippians 4:10–13 regarding his attitude toward contentment and God's provision. Note what you learn.

_____

_____

Sometimes we can fall into the mistaken mindset that when we follow faithfully after God, find refuge in His providential care, and obey His commands, we will not encounter hardship or trials. Read 2 Corinthians 11:23–28, and note Paul's severe hardships and the extraordinary persecution he endured as a follower and servant of Christ. Recap Paul's experiences below.

_____

_____

I cannot think of another more dedicated servant of our Lord than the apostle Paul. Yet, he endured many hardships. He had times when he went hungry. He spent time in prison and was even severely beaten. Through it all, Paul learned to be content, regardless of his circumstances. He persevered. He was fruitful in his service, and he had a rich relationship with the Lord that carried him through every bit of suffering he endured.

When Ruth sat before Boaz on the threshing floor, she and Naomi had no one to provide for them except Ruth herself. She was needy, and although a husband would not guarantee she would never again struggle to make ends meet, marriage would ensure Ruth was no longer alone and no longer on her own. In that culture, a man had the full responsibility of providing for his family. A husband meant a source of provision and care that a widow simply did not possess.

What title does Isaiah 54:5 ascribe to the Lord? _____

Ruth's ultimate provider was her Maker, the Lord Almighty. Read the following Scriptures and note what each says about God's provision for us as His people.

Isaiah 46:4: _____

Matthew 6:25–33: _____

_____

_____

Write Proverbs 3:5–6 below:

_____

_____

_____

WEEK FOUR

What does all of this mean for us? What provision can we count on as believers in Christ who, like Ruth, have found refuge under His *kanaph*? The apostle Paul's experiences help us understand that our own experience of having our needs met has more to do with our perspective than the abundance of our comfort or possessions. We can be content in all circumstances. More than any physical comfort or monetary provision, we need Jesus. He is our Sustainer (Isaiah 46:4). Whether we have plenty or are poor and hungry, we can "do all things" through Christ who strengthens us (Philippians 4:13). When we rely on the Lord and seek Him above all our physical needs, the Lord guides us and provides the things we need. Life may not always be comfortable and it may not be easy, but His presence with us

> More than any physical comfort or monetary provision, we need Jesus.

guides us. Our Maker is like a loving and caring husband who is attentive to and provides for our needs (Isaiah 54:5). Read Psalm 46:1–4 again, and look closely at verse 4. Why do you think a river's streams would make a city glad?

_____

_____

Streams provide water for humans, livestock, and trees and plants. They can be a source of drinking water and irrigation for crops. Streams bring life to a city and to those who live there. As we consider God's provision, there is a spring that is even more important to our well-being than a physical spring. As we wrap up this lesson, I want to draw your attention to a continual, life-giving source of refreshment that we possess as believers in Jesus. Jesus says it is a "spring of water welling up to eternal life" (John 4:14).

Read John 4:13–14. Who gives this spring of water? _____

Now read Jeremiah 2:13. What do you think the difference is between a spring of living water and a cistern? Look up the definitions of *cistern* and *spring of water* if you need help compiling your answer.

_____

_____

Read John 7:37–38. For those who believe in Jesus, from where did He say the living water will flow? _____

Read Ephesians 1:13–14. When do you receive the Holy Spirit? _____

_____

Now to wrap this up, read Romans 8:5–11. What does the Spirit provide to us?

_____

The living water Jesus gives (John 4:14) to those who believe in Him flows from within us (John 7:38). This wellspring within us is the Holy Spirit, who we receive when we believe the message of salvation through Jesus (Ephesians 1:13). God the Father sent God the Son to die for us so we could have eternal life. God the Holy Spirit indwells us, and His presence within us is the guarantee that when our time on this earth is complete, we will have a place in our eternal home (Ephesians 1:14) with our Lord. Our future is not uncertain. His Spirit is with us through every trial and struggle of this life, and when we transfer our residence to our eternal home, we can look forward to drinking freely of His Spirit in a more glorious way than we can ever imagine. For those who find refuge in God through faith in Jesus, His Spirit is the greatest expression of His glorious provision for His people. Refuge means provision—in Ruth's day as well as for us today.

|

Refuge Means Peace

He says, "Be still, and know that I am God; I will be exalted among the nations, I will be exalted in the earth."

PSALM 46:10

So far this week, we have focused on the security and provision God provides when we find refuge under His *kanaph* through faith in Jesus. Today, I want to focus on another benefit we experience when we take refuge in God through faith in Christ—the peace of God.

Jesus is the Prince of Peace (Isaiah 9:6). According to John 14:27, what does Jesus give us as His followers?

_____

You can have the peace of God. Let that rest on you for a moment. As we begin today, ask God to help you grasp the depth of His peace.

According to Galatians 5:22, what is the source of godly peace?

_____

When the Spirit takes up residence within us as believers in Jesus, we begin to produce the fruit of the Spirit, which includes peace. Godly peace. It is a peace that calms us and sustains us, regardless of our circumstances. Through faith in Jesus, we can have a sense of wellness and wholeness that enables us to rest our hope and lay our fears firmly in the hands of the One who is in control of all and knows all.

As we begin today, let's look at an example from Scripture of Jesus displaying His peace so we can have a better understanding of what godly peace looks like as we navigate our own difficult circumstances. Keep in mind that these were real people, and it was a real situation. Read the entire story in John 11:1–45. Note verses that depict Jesus displaying peace amid the chaos and grief around Him.

Why do you think Jesus was able to have peace despite the death of his beloved friend, Lazarus, and the cries and frustrations of Mary and Martha? (Hint: vv. 9–11.)

Jesus knew He would raise Lazarus from the dead. He knew God would be glorified through those frightening and sad circumstances. He knew the outcome from the beginning and had a purpose for His delayed return when his friend was sick.

When we find refuge under God's wings (Ruth 2:12) through faith in Jesus, we are filled with the peace of God the Son through the indwelling of God the Spirit. The Sovereign One who knows all things past, present, and future is with us through every situation we face. We don't have to fret when our struggles make the future seem uncertain. We can rest in God's providential care because we are loved by Jesus, just as Lazarus, Mary, and Martha were loved by Jesus (John 11:5). He doesn't always act when we expect (Mary and Martha were pretty upset with Jesus's timing), and He doesn't always revive that which we have lost. However, our Kinsman-Redeemer does care for us, and He is with us through the ups and downs of this life.

> The Sovereign One who knows all things past, present, and future is with us through every situation we face.

Marrying Boaz meant Ruth would never again be alone or on her own. Seeking refuge through our Kinsman-Redeemer means we are never alone and we never have to navigate this life on our own. Jesus gives us His peace—the peace of God. When God seems slow to come to our rescue, as with Lazarus, we can rest assured there is a purpose for His delay. When there doesn't seem to be an answer to our problems, we can know that our hope rests securely in a God who is able to accomplish His purposes in our lives. In fact, Ruth's entire story is an illustration of God's ability to accomplish His purposes. His peace is available to us regardless of the circumstances we face.

Take a moment to reflect on Lazarus's story and what you have learned so far about Ruth's story. Pray and ask God to help you draw peace from an awareness of His providential care for you.

As I began writing this lesson, God gave me a powerful illustration of what happens when we walk with Him along life's sometimes difficult path. My husband, Mark, and I were doing some yard work at our lake house. Our property is located on a cove of the lake, and part of our yard's perimeter runs along a ravine. We were cleaning out some debris along the edge of the ravine and came across a trail the deer use to cross from the other side of the gully into our unfenced yard. They come into our yard early in the mornings to seek out any bird seed the messy birds have scattered around our bird feeder. Mark and I decided to attempt walking the trail and were surprised by how steep and slippery it was because of pine needles and fallen leaves. The next morning, a bunch of deer (one had a fawn!) predictably appeared at the top of the trail on their usual morning walk to our bird feeder. One by one, even the fawn, they easily came up the trail into the yard. That morning's Bible reading landed me on Psalm 18.

Read Psalm 18:30–33 to see what God so clearly spoke to my heart that morning.

What does verse 30 tell us about God's ways, even when we don't understand them?

_____

What does He do for those who take refuge in Him (v. 30)?

_____

Reflect on our Day One lesson this week as you note the truth of verse 32:

_____

Drum roll, please! What does God make our feet like as he causes us to stand on the heights?

_____

Isn't that fabulous? Mark and I were only able to navigate that slippery slope by hanging on tightly to trees and slowly securing our feet on tree roots and brush as we precariously went down and then back up the ravine. Those deer were sure footed, easily making their daily trek up into our yard.

Look at Psalm 18:33 from the Amplified Classic Edition of the Bible:

> *He makes my feet like hinds' feet [able to stand firmly or make progress on the dangerous heights of testing and trouble]; He sets me securely upon my high places.*

When we find refuge in our Lord, He is with us. He shields us. He arms us with strength and keeps our way secure. He makes our feet like the feet of a deer so that we are able to stand firmly and make progress along the "dangerous heights of testing and trouble" this life sometimes brings our way. Because we find refuge in Him, we stand on heights as overcomers, sure footed even amid slippery, troublesome terrain.

When we find refuge in our Lord, He gives us peace. His peace.

WEEK FOUR | DAY FOUR

Refuge Means Mercy

> *"Surely goodness and mercy shall follow me all the days of my life, and I shall dwell in the house of the LORD forever."*
>
> PSALM 23:6 (ESV)

Both the book of Ruth and Psalm 23 speak of God's providence. Our Lord has an infinite ability to accomplish His purposes on earth and in our lives. Therefore, He is able to care for us and meet our needs. Begin today by reading all of

Psalm 23, and in your own words, note some of the ways our Lord and Shepherd meets the needs of those who find refuge in Him.

_____

_____

_____

According to verse 6, what will follow us all the days of our lives?

_____

Your version of Scripture may say "goodness and love," some say "goodness and mercy," and some say "goodness and faithfulness." Love and faithfulness are related to mercy and are expressions of God's mercy, so we will use the English Standard Version's interpretation and focus on the term *mercy*. When thinking of God's mercy, let's use a simple definition.

> **Mercy:** When God gives us what we need, rather than what we deserve.

God's mercy isn't just an act of God, but reflects His just, kind, compassionate, and faithful nature. *Easton's Bible Dictionary* speaks of God's nature this way: "God is not sometimes merciful and sometimes just, but He is eternally infinitely just and merciful."[34] In other words, we can count on God to always be just and always be merciful.

God provided insight into some of the ways He expresses His merciful and just character when He proclaimed His name to Moses on Mount Sanai. Now, most of us are at least familiar with the Ten Commandments, which were written by the finger of God on tablets of stone. But you may not know that Moses broke the original stone tablets. (Yep, he did. See Exodus 32:19.) Afterward, the Lord told Moses to chisel out two replacement stones (a fitting consequence if you ask me) and to meet Him on Mount Sinai so He could once again write on them. God described His merciful and just nature during that encounter with Moses on the mountain.

Read Exodus 34:1–7, and note what God proclaimed about Himself in verses 6–7.

_____

_____

_____

God is compassionate and slow to anger. He forgives wickedness, rebellion, and sin, yet "He does not leave the guilty unpunished." At first glance, there seems to be some contradiction there. Are you wondering how God can forgive wickedness and sin but never leave the guilty unpunished? I certainly have sinned, and when compared with God's standards, I am guilty of falling far short. None of us can keep all of God's commands and laws. Yet we can count on God to forgive; to rightly dispense punishment (as in Moses's chiseling assignment!); and to treat people fairly, rightly, and equitably. God is always just, and that means He cannot ignore sin or be inconsistent with dispensing consequences for wickedness, rebellion, and sin.

According to Romans 6:23, what is the punishment for sin? _____

Yet what is the gift of God? _____

In this simple verse in Romans, the complex quandary of how God can be both "infinitely just and merciful" is solved with the death of his Son, Jesus. Our sin and rebellion have earned us death. That is the punishment we deserve. And Jesus took that punishment upon Himself so that we could experience the fullness of God's mercy.

How did God demonstrate His love for us, according to Romans 5:8?

_____

We experience God's mercy only because Jesus took the punishment for our sins. Jesus didn't just die for you. He died in your place. He took upon Himself the punishment you deserve for every sin you have committed and ever will commit. He took the punishment that was necessary for God's justice to be carried out in response to your "wickedness, rebellion, and sin." And because He did, you experienced God's mercy. Jesus was and is your substitute on the cross. In Christ, we find the perfect expression of God's mercy and justice.

> In Christ, we find the perfect expression of God's mercy and justice.

What does Micah 7:18 tell us about God?

_____

God delights to show mercy. And His mercy is expressed whenever He provides what we need rather than what we deserve. Let that rest on you for a moment.

What are some ways God has met your personal needs?

_____

_____

WEEK FOUR

God cares for us. He shepherds us. He provides for our deepest needs. He even provided His Son to die so we could have eternal life. That is unfathomable mercy.

Mercy is what Ruth was seeking as she sat on the threshing floor before Boaz—someone to compassionately care for her, provide for her, shelter her, and love her. As a kinsman-redeemer, Boaz would take on the role of her caretaker. As believers in Jesus, our Lord mercifully cares for us like a shepherd caring for his sheep, just as Psalm 23 conveys.

Read and consider the Shepherd's care conveyed in each line of Psalm 23. Consider the ways God has expressed His merciful care for you, as mentioned in the psalm. It is easier to be specific when we focus our attention on a narrow time frame. So as you pray and reflect, focus on your life's circumstances over the past three months as you answer the questions.

The Lord is your shepherd. Reflect on His faithful care for you.

Read verse 1. How has God met your financial, physical, or emotional needs the past three months?

_____

Read verses 2–3. How has God provided rest, refreshment, and guidance?

_____

Read verse 4. How has God's presence sustained you and His discipline comforted you?

_____

Read verse 5. Have you been comforted by the Lord's presence or experienced some sort of healing or abundance?

Read verse 6. How has knowledge of your eternal security in Christ given you peace and hope?

Now read through Psalm 23 again slowly, reflecting on the notes you have made as you read.

God is your refuge. He is your Shepherd. He loves you. His goodness and mercy will follow you the rest of your days, and you will indeed dwell in His eternal house forever and ever.

Mercy.

WEEK FOUR | DAY FIVE

Personal Application

Surely goodness and mercy shall follow me all the days of my life, and I shall dwell in the house of the LORD forever.

PSALM 23:6 (ESV)

As we begin this lesson, my heart is full. As I mentioned before, our family is preparing for my daughter's upcoming wedding. Mark and I just arrived home from New York after attending a wedding shower with Bri's soon-to-be extended family. Every person at the shower seemed to be genuinely excited about the union of these two young people, and they had clearly embraced our daughter as a new member of their fun-loving, Italian family. This mother of the bride couldn't be happier to see the loving support she will have from her future in-laws. We all need support as we navigate the ups and, especially, the downs of this life.

Thankfully, when we take refuge in God's redeeming love, we become a part of His family, and we never have to walk through life alone. The Lord is our shepherd, and we can find security, provision, peace, and mercy under His divine, loving care.

Application From Day One

In Day One's lesson, we closed by focusing on our eternal security as believers in Jesus. I asked you to read Revelation 21:1–5, which gives us a glimpse of the glorious eternal life that one day awaits us. Reread Revelation 21:1–5.

What will the Lord declare when the New Jerusalem replaces our currently decaying earth (v. 5)?

Here's what's on my heart today regarding these passages. If you or a loved one struggles with chronic pain or some sort of debilitating illness, our God will provide new spiritual bodies in our eternal home. If your loved one has a mental illness or severe character flaws but places their faith in Jesus, one day you will have the opportunity to meet them in our eternal home as the person God originally designed them to be, not as they behaved while on this earth. The mistakes and failings of this life will pass away. The pain and suffering will be gone. Weaknesses will disappear. Offenses will seem like distant memories.

Did someone come to mind as you read those words? Do you struggle to forgive someone for offenses or wrongs that have been done to you or a loved one? Do you know someone who struggles with physical or mental illness and has not yet accepted Jesus as Savior? Take a moment right now to pray God would woo each of those people into a saving relationship with Jesus Christ. Share your faith stories. Share what it means to believe in Jesus. Pray for the opportunity to meet them in eternal glory without the imperfections that have dominated their time on this earth. This life is temporary. This life's order of things will pass away, and there will be no more crying or pain (v. 4). Our Creator God will make all things new! Those words are trustworthy and true (v. 5).

Note anything you sense God whispering to your heart.

_____

_____

_____

Application From Day Two

In Day Two we looked at the truths and warnings about our attitude toward wealth and possessions as outlined in 1 Timothy 6:3–19. Look back at the warnings you noted (page 66). Is there any evidence of these wrong attitudes in your life? If so, write a prayer below and ask God to change your heart. If not, write a prayer and ask God to help guard your heart.

_____

_____

_____

_____

Application From Day Three

How does an awareness of God's providence—His infinite ability to accomplish His purposes on earth and in your life—and an awareness of the eternal life that awaits us after our time on this life is through enable you to have peace, regardless of your circumstances?

_____

Now, here is a more pointed question: What situation or circumstance in your life right now is causing you to worry or fret?

_____

Do you believe God is able to accomplish His purposes in that situation? _____

What does Romans 8:28–29 tell you God does for those who love God?

_____

On the lines below, write a prayer to God right now, entrusting the situation that causes you to fret or worry to His providential care.

_____

_____

_____

_____

Application From Day Four

Write a definition of *mercy* in your own words.

_____

Think of the relationship in your life that causes you the most stress or frustration. What does mercy look like in that relationship? _____

_____

_____

_____

Ask God to help you do just that.

Week 5

Judicious Decisions

Dawning Providence

Stay here for the night, and in the morning if he wants to do his duty as your guardian-redeemer, good; let him redeem you. But if he is not willing, as surely as the LORD lives I will do it. Lie here until morning.

RUTH 3:13

After a week spent studying outside the book of Ruth, let's refresh our memories before moving on with the story of this budding romance between a young widow and a not-so-young landowner living in Bethlehem, Judah.

Slowly and thoughtfully read Ruth 3:1–9, reflecting on all that you have learned so far about the story of Naomi, Ruth, and Boaz. Note any details in the text that have come to life for you because of your studies.

_____

_____

The notes you have just made are evidence of some of the benefits we receive when we practice the spiritual discipline of studying God's Word. We learn. Scripture comes to life. Truths take on greater meaning. Most of all, God speaks to us as He applies His Word to our everyday situations and struggles. So let's once again dig into Ruth's story. When we last saw her, Ruth was sitting in the dark, positioned at Boaz's uncovered feet at the end of a grain pile on the town's public fleshing floor.

Look at Ruth 3:9 again.

Ruth's response to Boaz was a carefully crafted marriage proposal: "Spread the corner of your garment over me" was a "vivid expression for providing protection, warmth and fellowship. The phrase spoke eloquently of marriage."[35] Boaz understood her request and her reasons for the proposal. Do you remember what we learned about the role of the guardian-redeemer?

If needed, look back at pages 56 and 59 of our study to refresh your memory before moving forward.

As Boaz absorbed all that Ruth was proposing, he seemed to be touched by her request. Look closely at Ruth 3:10. What seemed to surprise Boaz most, and how did he describe her actions?

There are a few dynamics in the situation that probably prompted Boaz's response. First, Ruth was not just seeking a husband for herself in order to carry on Mahlon's family line. Elimelek's family line had been extinguished when both sons died. Ruth's proposal would provide descendants for Naomi and Elimelek, not just for her and Mahlon. Ruth's actions constituted a beautiful act of unselfish, loving kindness toward her mother-in-law.

Look back at Ruth 2:10–12. When Ruth originally asked Boaz why she had found such favor with him, what had Boaz heard about Ruth that prompted him to treat her with such kindness when she began working in his field (v. 11)?

Kindness is devotion and love in action, and it appears to have been a character trait Ruth displayed often. In fact, it has been a theme in our study. In Ruth 1:9, Naomi prayed God would grant Ruth the same kindness she had apparently expressed toward Naomi and her two sons after the loss of Elimelek. As Ruth sat boldly before Boaz, asking him to marry her and provide a means of continuing Elimelek's family line, her courage was fueled by her apparent love and concern for Naomi. Let's see what kindnesses Boaz offered Ruth in return.

Read Ruth 3:7–13.

As I read Ruth's proposal to Boaz, it occurred to me that she was asking Boaz to become the person through whom God would answer the prayer he had so graciously prayed over Ruth at their very first meeting. Look back at Ruth 2:12, and note what Boaz asked God to do for Ruth:

Boaz had the opportunity to be a participant in God's providential work in Ruth's life. When he originally said that prayer for Ruth, it probably never occurred to him that the Lord would use him as the vessel through whom He "richly rewarded" the widow from Moab for her loving kindness toward Naomi.

Boaz was willing to marry Ruth and faithfully act on his responsibility as a guardian-redeemer for Elimelek's family. I imagine Ruth could hardly contain her relief as Boaz said he would do all she asked. But her relief probably morphed into trepidation as he explained that there was another man who was a closer male relative. In other words, Ruth might just end up married off to a man she hadn't yet met—a man who was not the kind "man of standing" who had continually shown her kindness as she worked in his fields.

What thoughts do you think might have been racing through Ruth's mind as Boaz explained the complexity of the situation?

Scripture doesn't tell us Ruth's thoughts, but if it were me, I would have started praying as soon as I heard a "but" in Boaz's voice. Boaz assured Ruth that he would indeed act as her guardian-redeemer if the other relative was not willing to do so. Then he encouraged her to stay there on the threshing floor until morning.

Read Ruth 3:14. Ruth agreed to stay, but what did she do before it became light enough for anyone to recognize her?

The people of Bethlehem may have known that Ruth was "a woman of noble character" (v. 11), but she and Boaz did not leave any opportunity for Ruth's intentions to become the talk of that small town. As Boaz expressed his concern, "No one must know that a woman came to the threshing floor" and Ruth prepared to exit quickly, Boaz extended one more kindness to the young widow who had captured his respect (and I suspect his heart) from their first meeting back in his grain field.

To end today's lesson, read Ruth 3:15, and note what Boaz gave Ruth before they both quickly left the threshing floor.

We aren't told what measure of grain was used, but whatever it was, I imagine Ruth was grateful. Perhaps if anyone had noticed her leaving the threshing floor early that morning, they would have assumed she had gone there for grain, not to proposition Boaz. Whatever the measure, Ruth went home with six of them. I don't know how full her shawl was on that walk back to her home that morning, but as sun began to rise there in Bethlehem, Ruth was embarking on the dawn of God's providential purposes for herself, for her beloved mother-in-law, and for Boaz.

WEEK FIVE · DAY TWO

The Wait

*Then Naomi said, "Wait, my daughter, until you find out what happens. For
the man will not rest until the matter is settled today."*

RUTH 3:18

*I*n our last lesson, we witnessed the intensely important meeting between Ruth and
Boaz on Bethlehem's threshing floor. Ruth had risked her reputation and her dignity
to approach Boaz boldly during the night with the proposal that had the potential to
change her life. Marriage to Boaz would also provide life-sustaining shelter and provision
for Naomi. It could eventually provide an heir to continue Elimelek's family line.

Boaz had been willing to act as the guardian-redeemer, but a closer relative had first dibs,
so to speak, for that position. As Ruth made her way home in the wee hours of the morning, I imagine the burden of carrying six measures of barley in her shawl was nothing compared to the weight of the uncertainty surrounding her circumstances. Would Ruth soon
be married to Boaz, or would she be thrust into a lifelong union with a man she had never
even met? I suspect that was a long, lonely walk home from the threshing floor.

Read Ruth 3:16–17.

What question did Naomi ask Ruth as she arrived home?

_____

The question may vary slightly depending on your version of Scripture. My NIV translates
the question, "How did it go, my daughter?" whereas the NKJV states it, "Is that you, my
daughter?" However, in Hebrew, the text says, "Who are you?" and "in this context Naomi
is clearly not asking for Ruth's identity. Here the question has the semantic force 'Are
you his wife?'"[36] I imagine the question struck Ruth like a piercing arrow to the heart. At
that moment, Ruth had no idea whose wife she was destined to become. It was probably

the question she had pondered the entire walk home. With that question, I surmise the courage and strength Ruth had maintained the prior evening crumbled as she relayed the series of events to Naomi.

Please read Ruth 3:18. What does Naomi say to Ruth?

_____

I imagine Naomi's words were in response to a series of anxiety-filled questions from a weary and troubled Ruth. After all, she knew nothing about this mysterious close relative of Naomi's. Why hadn't Naomi mentioned him? Did Naomi avoid mentioning him because he would not be a suitable husband? Would he be kind to Ruth and Naomi? Did he live in Bethlehem? Would Ruth's marriage to this unknown relative require them to leave the town where Ruth was probably just beginning to feel at home? Perhaps Ruth echoed her beloved mother-in-law's own question: Who am I going to become? Naomi urged Ruth not to panic or fret and to wait for Boaz to handle it, for he would not "rest until the matter is settled," and Naomi was confident that Boaz would handle it that day.

The wait. Regardless of how long we have followed the Lord, the waits of our lives are challenging. For Ruth, that day's events promised to be of utmost importance to her future—and of utmost importance to Naomi's future. When the results for which we wait have the potential to change the course of our lives, a wait can seem agonizingly cruel.

When I was in my thirties, I had an incident that presented much like a stroke and resulted in numbness and weakness in my left arm. After an emergency room visit that yielded no answers, I was referred to a neurologist who, after an examination and some initial tests, confidently offered a diagnosis of some form of multiple sclerosis. He expressed uncertainty as to the type, but even though my tests were inconclusive, he left no room for any other explanation for

> Regardless of how long we have followed the Lord, the waits of our lives are challenging.

the symptoms as he handed me a business card for a specialist. I was devastated. That doctor's diagnosis replayed in my head several times each day. The inconclusive tests troubled me greatly as I clung to any possibility that he was wrong. At the suggestion of a friend, I sought out a doctor of internal medicine to review my case and help me navigate the process of confirming the daunting diagnosis. Unfortunately, I had to wait almost a month for an appointment. That month-long wait seemed like a year. My imagination ran wild with worst-case scenarios. It was an agonizingly cruel wait. Each day I faced an exhausting struggle to wrestle down fear regarding my future. That internist studied my tests and, on a hunch, ordered an MRI on my neck—the only upper-body part that had not already been scanned. It turns out a disk in my cervical spine was compressing my spinal cord. Now, the surgery and long path to recovery were not easy, but I am thankful for the experience that now enables me to better empathize with women like Ruth who must wait for news that could alter the course of their lives.

Have you ever experienced a difficult time of waiting for news that would affect your future or the future of a loved one? How does your experience help you better understand some of the emotions Ruth might have been experiencing as she waited for the outcome of Boaz's meeting?

We all will experience some seasons of wait, whether a day, a month, or possibly even years. As we seek to learn from Naomi's journey through the book of Ruth, let's see what we can glean from other passages in our Bibles regarding how we navigate a wait.

Read Psalm 27:13–14. Regardless of the circumstances, on whom do we truly wait?

What do you learn about longer seasons of extended wait from Isaiah 40:29–31?

Do you remember the passages we read in Habakkuk earlier in our study? If you recall, the Lord told Habakkuk that Israel's hardship had a purpose and would eventually come to an end. The Lord's words to Habakkuk are a good reminder to us when we are waiting for God to carry out His plans in our lives as well. What did God say to Habakkuk in Habakkuk 2:3?

God had a plan, but His work had an appointed time, and the people had to wait. In fact, look at Habakkuk 1:5. What did God tell Habakkuk about His plans?

What does Isaiah 55:8–9 tell us about God's plans?

God is always at His work (John 5:17), but sometimes we must wait for His plans to unfold. That day in Bethlehem, Ruth was waiting for Boaz to meet with Mr. Mystery Relative, but ultimately, she was waiting on the Lord to accomplish His purpose. Our God was able to orchestrate His desired outcome for Ruth, much like He is able to bring about His desired outcome in our lives today. When we look to Him and trust Him through our waits, our strength is renewed such that we overcome our discouragement and challenges to eventually rise like eagles soaring over the mountains (Isaiah 40:31). There will be times when God seems silent or His action seems to take longer than we could have ever anticipated. But we can count on God's providence—His infinite ability to accomplish His purposes on earth and in our individual lives. Although His plan may seem to "linger, wait for it" (Habakkuk 2:3). The Lord's purposes may not always result in the outcome we want. He may have a plan in the works that we would not believe, even if we were told (Habakkuk 1:5). He may not do what we expect, and we will not always understand His ways (Isaiah 55:8–9), but we can count on the fact that He is at work.

Wait for Him. Trust Him. Seek Him.

We don't know any details about how Ruth spent the day as she waited for the conclusion of Boaz's meeting, but her answer was not delayed. As we will see in tomorrow's lesson, Boaz was quick to act, and the Lord was moving swiftly that day at Bethlehem's gate.

Unsandaled Mr. So-and-So

*Meanwhile Boaz went up to the town gate and sat down there just as the
guardian-redeemer he had mentioned came along.*

RUTH 4:1A

In our last lesson, Ruth returned home from her night on the threshing room floor carrying a shawl full of barley and a suspense-filled account of her encounter with her potential kinsman-redeemer. Ruth shared the unfortunate news that there was another kinsman who had the first right to marry Ruth. Ruth's stress over that unexpected information seemed evident as Naomi encouraged her to wait until Boaz settled the matter. As Ruth and Naomi waited to see how their future years in Bethlehem might unfold, Boaz was already busy at Bethlehem's city gate.

Read Ruth 4:1–2.

Who came along just as Boaz took a seat at the town gate?

_____

In ancient Israel the town gates were constructed of lookout towers with a series of rooms on either side of the gate. They served as a gathering place for the citizens and the place where judicial business for the community was conducted.[37] Boaz sat down, probably giving the signal that he was there at the gate on judicial business. Lo and behold, along came the very man with whom Boaz wanted to meet. That, my friend, is called God's providence.

According to verse 1, how did Boaz address the unnamed kinsman who sat down with him at this official meeting at the town gate?

_____

Interestingly, although Boaz "probably would have actually used the man's name," the storyteller who wrote the book of Ruth apparently wanted to "suppress the name."[38] In effect, the writer of this story referred to the man who was unwilling to redeem the land as "Mr. So-and-So."[39] According to *The Jewish Study Bible*, the Mr. So-and-So title may have been chosen as an expression of "the narrator's disapproval of the man's behavior."[40]

According to verse 2, who else was at the judicial hearing there at the city gate?

Boaz probably had to round up ten elders. In quite the take-charge manner, he instructed the town leaders to take their seats, "and they did so" as the meeting commenced. Those elders may have been the official witnesses, but God was clearly presiding over that official meeting at Bethlehem's city gate.

Read Ruth 4:3. How did Boaz initially describe the situation?

Widows were not allowed to own property, so it is doubtful that Naomi was actually selling the family property. After all, if she and Ruth could work the family farm, there would have been no reason for Ruth to glean in Boaz's field. Let's do a little digging. What insight into Naomi and Ruth's plight do you gain from God's instructions recorded in Leviticus 25:25–27?

Scripture doesn't provide details about Elimelek's economic status when he lived in Bethlehem, but family land was considered an Israelite's most valuable asset, and each family's allotment of land was supposed to remain within their family. It is likely that Elimelek either leased his family's property or sold it before he and Naomi made the tragic decision to move to Moab over a decade earlier. It "appears the land had fallen into the hands of someone outside the family."[41] Boaz was offering Mr. So-and So the opportunity to redeem what Elimelek sold.

Let's see how that meeting unfolded. Now read Ruth 4:4.

The Net Bible translates Boaz's opening words in verse 4 as, "So I am legally informing you: Acquire it before those sitting here and before the leaders of my people!"[42] In this interpretation, there is an exclamation point at the end of the sentence and Boaz seemed much more formal with his delivery. This is how I envision the scenario at the city gate that day. Boaz was there on official business, and he was making sure the elders witnessed this very important legal proceeding. I imagine Boaz worked hard to disguise his disappointment when Mr. So-and-So said he would redeem Elimelek's family land.

Let's see what happened next. Please read Ruth 4:5.

Boaz made sure the potential redeemer knew all the details involved in the transaction before he finalized his legal commitment. Now, I am simply speculating, but I can't help but wonder if Boaz delivered those words in a slow, controlled monotone in an effort to disguise his desire to marry Ruth himself.

Now read Ruth 4:6–8.

What did Mr. So-and-So do to solidify his decision?

Do you remember what we learned about the stigma that followed the family of a man who refused to redeem his dead relative's land by marrying his widow? Look again at Deuteronomy 25:7–10, and note the name by which that family would then be identified.

What was the reason Mr. So-and-So said he could not redeem Elimelek's family land (v. 6)?

When Mr. So-and-So discovered he would have to support both Ruth and Naomi and that Ruth's son would inherit land, possibly from both family lines, the whole kinsman-redeemer package was no longer appealing. As to the "Family of the Unsandaled" stigma mentioned in Deuteronomy 25, it is possible the stigma might still have lingered over this man's name at the writing of the book of Ruth.

As for Boaz, I suspect he had to choke down his emotions as the realization washed over him that he would soon be the husband of that hardworking "woman of noble character" (Ruth 3:11) who caught his eye from the very first day he saw her gleaning in his barley field. Don't you just love a good love story?

Tomorrow we will see how the meeting at the city gate concluded. I wonder if Boaz had a joyful skip in his own sandaled step as the meeting adjourned and he headed toward Naomi's house to share the good news with his soon-to-be bride.

WEEK FIVE | DAY FOUR

Building a Legacy

May the LORD make the woman who is coming into your home like Rachel and Leah, who together built up the family of Israel. May you have standing in Ephrathah and be famous in Bethlehem.

RUTH 4:11B

The scene at Bethlehem's gate in yesterday's lesson concluded with Mr. So-and-So removing his sandal as he relinquished his option to redeem Elimelek's family land and marry Ruth. The suspenseful judicial hearing was over, and Boaz and Ruth were to be married.

Refresh your memory by rereading Ruth 4:1–8.

Now, let's see how Boaz ended that life-changing official meeting. Please read Ruth 4:9–10.

In addition to Elimelek's family land, what else was protected by the transaction (v. 10)?

_____

Elimelek's land would remain in the family when it was passed on to the firstborn son of Boaz and Ruth. But Boaz's redemption of the land also ensured the family name would not be eliminated from history. The family legacy would remain intact. Obviously, the family name was preserved among the people living in Bethlehem, but God also saw fit to include their family's story in Scripture so that we still remember their names to this day.

Read Ruth 4:11–12. On the lines below, record the three prayers the elders prayed over Boaz at the conclusion of the meeting there at the city gate.

1). May the Lord make Ruth _____

_____

2). May Boaz have _____

_____.

3). Through the offspring the Lord gives you by Ruth, may your family _____

_____.

We will spend today exploring the significance of each of the elders' prayers.

The first prayer was for Ruth to be "like Rachel and Leah." Let's do an abbreviated Israelite history lesson to get a better understanding of that prayer. What did the elders say Rachel and Leah built up?

_____

The nation of Israel descended from a man named Jacob, who was the grandson of Abraham. Jacob had two wives, Rachel and Leah, who were sisters, and each of them had sons with Jacob. At his wives' request, he also had sons with two of the household servants (I know. It's mind blowing, huh? We won't go down that rabbit hole today.) Jacob had a total of twelve sons from his wives Rachel and Leah and the two servants. Jacob's name was eventually changed.

According to Genesis 32:28, what name was Jacob given later in his life?

_____

What were Israel's sons called (Genesis 49:28)? _____

Rachel and Leah are credited with "building up" the family of Israel, from whom all the Israelites descended. They were fruitful. The elders' prayer was probably a request for Ruth to be fruitful and multiply, building up Boaz's family as Rachel and Leah had built up Israel's family.

The second prayer was for Boaz himself. What two city names are mentioned in the prayer?

_____ and _____

Interestingly, Ephrathah—or Ephrath, depending on your version of the Bible—is another name for Bethlehem, and it means fruitfulness. The elders' prayer for Boaz was probably again focused on his fruitfulness (both in children and in wealth) and for his name to be remembered in Bethlehem. Boaz was indeed famous, not only in Bethlehem, but with everyone who reads Scripture today.

WEEK FIVE

In the elders' final prayer, the focus was on Boaz and Ruth's family line. Read Ruth 4:12 from the NASB1995 below:

> *Moreover, may your house be like the house of Perez whom Tamar bore to Judah, through the offspring which the L*ORD *will give you by this young woman.*

To understand the third prayer of the elders at Bethlehem's city gate that day, we need to know the story behind the house of Perez. Warning: this reading probably should have at least a PG-13 rating. Read all of Genesis 38, and fill in the blanks below:

> Boaz was indeed famous, not only in Bethlehem, but with everyone who reads Scripture today.

Who was Tamar's first husband, and how was he related to Judah (v. 6)?

_____

What happened to Er? _____

Which of Er's brothers was supposed to fulfill his brotherly duty to provide a son for his deceased brother, but did not? (We won't note the details of his betrayal, but let's just say he should have been considered worse than unsandaled.)

_____

What were the circumstances of Perez's birth?

_____

_____

Mentioning the family of Perez and the . . . umm . . . union of Judah and Tamar seems like a strange choice, doesn't it? I suspect the elders' prayer was related to Perez's descendants rather than the actions of his parents. But Tamar's levirate marriage certainly is an interesting common element considering the circumstances.

Look at 1 Chronicles 2:5. What were the names of Perez's two sons?

_____ and _____

Now read 1 Chronicles 2:9–12. What was Perez's connection to Boaz?

_____

Look back at Ruth 2:1, and note how Boaz was originally identified in the book of Ruth.

A clan was a family unit within a tribe. That means Perez was the ancestor of both Elimelek and Boaz. As the judicial gathering at Bethlehem's gate concluded, the elders prayed for Ruth to be fruitful and for Boaz's name to remembered in Bethlehem, and perhaps their mention of the house of Perez was a prayer for the family of this union to produce some more leaders and men of great standing in Israel's future. As we will see in the lessons to come, God answered every one of those elders' prayers. Boaz and Ruth didn't just build a family, God used them to build a legacy that still affects the world today.

WEEK FIVE   DAY FIVE

Personal Application

Application from Day One

Ruth displayed tremendous personal character as she worked hard gleaning and gathering in Boaz's fields. To refresh your memory, how is Ruth described in 3:11?

Ruth was indeed noble, but she was also courageous. She risked her reputation as she boldly uncovered Boaz's feet and spent the night there beside him on the threshing floor. There was a chance that Boaz would misunderstand her motives. Not only that, but Boaz could have rejected her request. Ruth could have been humiliated in front all the men who were there on the town threshing floor. Sometimes, to follow God and be a part of His divine purposes, we must courageously risk humiliation or defeat.

Interestingly, some of the most courageous servants of our Lord also happen to be among the most humble and unassuming. God used Moses to deliver his people from slavery and lead them through the wilderness for forty years. I am certainly not putting Ruth on the same level with Moses, but I think Moses's battle with insecurity and inadequacy is relatable for most of us. Let's see how he is described in the passages listed below.

Exodus 4:10 _____

_____

Numbers 12:3 _____

Deuteronomy 34:10–12 _____

_____

Moses didn't feel qualified. He risked humiliation when he told the Israelites he was the man God chose to deliver them from slavery. Yet Moses found the courage to follow God's instructions. As a result, the Israelites were freed, and "no one has ever shown the mighty power or performed the awesome deeds that Moses did in the sight of all Israel" (Deuteronomy 34:12).

Like Ruth, you may feel inferior to people around you (Ruth 2:13), or maybe like Moses, you don't think of yourself as eloquent and you fumble to say the right words when you are called on to speak. Here's the truth: God has an infinite ability to accomplish His purposes on earth and in your life. Moses was used mightily by God despite his weaknesses, and he can do the same with you.

Ruth was a Moabite widow approaching a man of great standing in her community with a marriage proposal. Ruth mustered up the courage to execute Naomi's plan, and Boaz responded favorably. On the lines below, take a moment to write a prayer and ask God to help you overcome fear or any sense of inadequacy and to find the courage to take risks as you follow Him.

_____

_____

_____

_____

Application from Day Two

Ruth had to wait for the outcome of Boaz's meeting to know whether she would be married to Boaz or Mr. So-and-So. Waits are challenging.

As you work on today's lesson, are you still waiting for God to answer a prayer? Is there something you have sensed God doing in your life, but the results of that work are still unclear to you? Look back at the passages we reviewed in this week's Day Two Lesson. Craft a prayer using some of those passages on the lines below. Ask God to help you trust Him with your deepest desires and most heartfelt prayers. Ask Him to help you rest under His *kanaph* as you endure your season of wait.

_____

_____

_____

_____

Application from Day Three and Four

The unsandaled Mr. So-and-So may have still carried the stigma of the "Family of the Unsandaled" (Deuteronomy 25:10) at the writing of the book of Ruth. In contrast, Boaz and Ruth are forever remembered among Jews and Christians because their story is recorded in Scripture. Our actions during our time on this earth determine how we are remembered by future generations. The mark we leave on this world is considered our legacy.

> Our actions during our time on this earth determine how we are remembered by future generations.

Think about a beloved parent or grandparent who is no longer alive. What do you remember most about this person?

_____

_____

Do you have any relatives of whom you do not have good memories? What do you remember most about that person?

_____

_____

What you have just written could be considered that person's legacy. Our personal achievements, the way we treat other people, and the manner in which we live out our faith before our families all contribute to the legacy we leave behind.

As you consider the legacy you will leave behind when your days on earth are complete, take a moment to consider the impact you want to have in the following areas.

Regarding the relationships you have with family members or close friends, how do you want to be remembered?

_____

_____

What do you want people to remember about the way you spend your time?

_____

_____

What do you want people to remember about the way you live out your faith?

_____

_____

Do you need to make any changes for the answers you just wrote down to become your legacy? If so, write a prayer asking God for the courage and strength to make those changes. If your answers are in line with your actions, write a prayer of thankfulness for the work God has done in you and the legacy He has enabled you to create.

_____

_____

_____

_____

May the Lord make you fruitful in every way, may your name be remembered favorably by your family, and may you leave behind a legacy of faith that continues for generations to come.

WEEK FIVE

Week 6

Redemption

The Wedding

So Boaz took Ruth and she became his wife. When he made love to her, the
LORD enabled her to conceive, and she gave birth to a son.

RUTH 4:13

When we closed Week Five, Boaz's official meeting with the elders and Mr. So-and-So at Bethlehem's city gate had adjourned, and the elders had pronounced blessings over the union of Boaz and Ruth. I suspect Boaz then quickly made his way to Naomi's house to inform his future mother-in-law and his bride-to-be of the good news that he and Ruth were to be married.

Now, I've mentioned that I am in the throes of planning my daughter's wedding, so, of course, I immediately wondered what kind of ceremony the future Mr. and Mrs. Boaz had to plan and when it took place. Unfortunately, there are no details of the events surrounding their marriage. However, there is a hint for us that the typical wedding rituals of the day did indeed take place.

Look at Ruth 4:13 at the top of the page, and fill in the blank below

So Boaz _____ Ruth and she became his wife (Ruth 4:13a).

According to *The New American Commentary*, this expression reflects the "specific cus-tom of the man taking (*laqah*) his wife to his house as part of the marriage ritual."[43] In ancient Israel, a groom would go and get his bride from her parents' home (or in this case, Naomi's home) to escort her to his house, which would then become the couple's home.[44] I thought it was interesting that, like many brides today, a bride in Israel wore a veil during the ceremony. In a bride's dressing room prior to the marriage ceremony, a groom would drop a veil over his bride's face and a blessing would be pronounced over her. The bless-ing was reminiscent of the blessing spoken over Rebekah when she agreed to become the wife of Abraham's son, Isaac.[45]

According to Genesis 24:60, what was that blessing?

_____

_____

The increasing to thousands part is a sweet blessing. Possessing "the cities of your ene-mies" part—well, let's just say that was a big deal back then, and I'm thankful most of us today do not have to be concerned with military battles for territory. Now, back to the wedding. The ceremonies in Ruth's day usually occurred at night, and they began with a procession that went from the bride's home to the groom's home. The dark path between their homes would be lit with oil lamps held by their wedding guests. There was music and singing along the way.[46] The ceremony itself was conducted under a wedding canopy called a *chupa*.[47] The name gives us an idea how the canopy was decorated because it means "to cover with garlands."[48] The canopy consisted of a large piece of decorated mate-rial made from silk, satin, or velvet, and it was supported by four firm poles.[49] I imagine the lights and the *chupa* with the garland created a simple yet beautiful setting for a wedding. Ruth probably also looked beautiful. Scripture gives us some hints as to her attire as she and Boaz celebrated their union. Note what you learn from the following passages about the bride's wedding attire.

Psalm 45 is noted as a wedding song. What do we learn about the bride's garments from verse 13?

_____

Isaiah 61:10: _____

Brides adorned themselves with jewelry, and Ruth may have worn a white embroidered gown. Boaz probably also wore special attire for their happy occasion. At Israelite weddings, a groom wore a white robe that symbolized purity and served as a reminder that the "new life on which he [was] about to embark must be pure and clean."[50] Interestingly, the bride and groom were not the only ones who wore special garments to a wedding ceremony in ancient Israel. The "host furnished wedding garments to all the guests."[51] I am thankful today's hosts are not required to provide wedding attire for all the guests. If that were the case, we would probably be trimming down that guest list considerably.

Like many wedding receptions of today, the celebration probably included music, dancing, and a feast. I am looking forward to that part of our upcoming celebration. The Fergusons enjoy big family meals, and at family weddings, we dance like no one is watching (they might wish they weren't!). In Ruth and Boaz's time, weddings "lasted for one to two weeks."[52] I like a good party, and I'm excited about seeing our out-of-town relatives, but I am glad our wedding guests will not be staying for weeks. Just sayin'.

As Ruth and Boaz stood under the *chupa* and recited whatever vows Israelites said to one another in those times, I find myself wondering if the realization that Ruth was officially becoming Boaz's wife caused her to ponder all the titles she had identified with since she first met Naomi and married her son back in Moab. Let's take a moment to review. Ruth had been a Moabite, perhaps a descendant of the Moabite king Eglon. After her first wedding, she became known as the wife of Mahlon and daughter-in-law of Elimelek and Naomi. We can safely assume that her marriage to an Israelite brought with it the stigma of being married to a man who descended from long-time Moabite enemies. Then, when her ten years of marriage to Mahlon failed to produce children, I would guess Ruth also carried the informal yet discouraging title of a barren woman. After Mahlon's tragic death, Ruth took on the dreaded title of widow.

During our study of the book of Ruth, we also discovered Ruth had some other titles she applied to herself. Read the passages below, and note how she identified herself.

Ruth 2:10: _____

Ruth 2:13: _____

As we consider all the titles Ruth carried, take a minute to consider the labels you have had during your lifetime. Maybe as a child you were called by a nickname. (Mine was Teapot when I was in elementary school. My teachers would sing "I'm a Little Teapot," and I would tilt on cue and pretend to pour from my hand like a teapot. It was all a lot of fun until I discovered the meaning of the word *stout*.) Like Ruth, perhaps your economic or social circumstances left you feeling less than people around you. Or, in contrast, if your family was wealthy or prestigious, you may have carried the label rich. You may be a daughter, sister, mother, or wife. On the lines below, note some of the labels or titles you have carried.

_____

_____

_____

Later this week, we will talk more about the new identity we have when we choose to find refuge under God's *kanaph*, but for now, just know that those labels, whether positive or negative, do not define you.

According to 2 Corinthians 5:17, what assurance do we have as believers in Jesus?

_____

That night in Bethlehem as Boaz and Ruth became one flesh (Genesis 2:24), the widowed foreigner, who considered her social standing to be lower than any servant in Boaz's field, became the wife of Boaz, the "man of standing" in their community. Her old identity was gone. No more gleaning in fields. No more struggling to provide for herself and her beloved mother-in-law. I suppose Ruth's wedding night brought her great joy, but it also brought her a fresh identity.

> I suppose Ruth's wedding night brought her great joy, but it also brought her a fresh identity.

Read Ruth 4:13 again.

After the festivities of the evening were complete and Boaz and Ruth consummated their marriage, what did the Lord do for Ruth and Boaz?

_____

I imagine it was a beautiful wedding that united two distinctly different lives. The heir for which the elders prayed and the one who stood to carry on Elimelek's family line was granted to Ruth. We don't know the reasons she and Mahlon never had children, but we do know that two lives became one and God granted the honorable Boaz and his noble wife, Ruth, a son. It was a fruitful union, indeed (Ruth 4:11).

WEEK SIX | DAY TWO

Lineage of a Son

The women living there said, "Naomi has a son!" And they named him Obed.
He was the father of Jesse, the father of David.

RUTH 4:17

oaz and Ruth were married, and the Lord blessed them with a fruitful union when the couple produced a son. Begin today by reading Ruth 4:13–17.

What name was given to Boaz and Ruth's baby boy?

_____

Eight days after little Obed was born, he would have been circumcised. Israelite boys were circumcised, according to instructions given to Abraham. Let's read God's instructions to Abraham in Genesis 17:1–13.

Who was to be circumcised (v. 10)? _____

What was the purpose of circumcision according to verse 11?

_____

Abraham was circumcised at the age of ninety-nine (Genesis 17:1), and from that day forward, every Israelite male was to be circumcised as a sign of the promises God made to Abraham and his descendants. The circumcision ceremony was called the *brit*, and it was at that ceremony that an Israelite boy was given his name. In fact, the brit was considered the most important religious event in the boy's life.[53] We can assume the people of Bethlehem who had been so familiar with Naomi and Ruth's story attended the brit for Boaz and Ruth's son and they all enjoyed a festive dinner afterward to celebrate the significant occasion.

WEEK SIX

Look closely at Ruth 4:17. Who named the baby? _____

What did Naomi's girlfriends in Bethlehem call little Obed in verse 14?

_____

At first glance, you might think the women were referring to Boaz because he served as Ruth's guardian-redeemer, but what is clarified in verse 15?

_____

According to the Jewish scholar and historian Josephus, Obed's name was chosen because the intention was for the child to become Naomi's caretaker in her old age, "for Obed in the Hebrew dialect signifies a servant."[54] The women referring to Obed as Naomi's kinsman-redeemer seemed strange to me. However, Naomi's friends seemed to be thinking in the context of little Obed fulfilling the role of heir to Naomi's son Mahlon. The little boy was the only one of Boaz and Ruth's children who would be considered Naomi's kin, and as her new closest relative, he would carry the responsibility for taking care of his grandmother later in life.

Scripture doesn't tell us much about the life Obed led or about his character traits. However, as the son of two noble, hardworking parents who were committed to serving their God as well as their families, I would like to think Obed lived up to his name.

Next, we will read the final verses in the book of Ruth. I feel a twinge of sadness as our time together studying this compelling story comes to a close. However, the ending of Ruth's story is far grander than anything we have studied so far. So, without further delay, please read Ruth 4:18–22 slowly and thoughtfully as you recall what you have learned about Boaz (and Elimelek's) family history.

What was the name of Obed's son? _____

What do you learn about Jesse from 1 Samuel 17:12–14?

_____

_____

In the time when Jesse's sons were growing up, the "days when the judges ruled" (Ruth 1:1) were over and Israel was under the rule of their first king, named Saul. He was a pretty terrible king, but that's a lesson for another time. The Lord told the prophet Samuel that He had chosen one of Jesse's sons to serve as king after Saul. Let's see which son God chose to succeed Saul.

Please read 1 Samuel 16:1–13. What did you learn about Jesse's son David?

_____

_____

Which of Jesse's sons is the only one mentioned in the final verse of the book of Ruth?

_____

Now read Psalm 89:3–4. What did the Lord tell David about the future of his lineage and throne?

_____

_____

The family of Obed's grandson David would be established forever, and David's throne would stand through all generations. Now look at what the prophet Isaiah said about a descendant of David who would reign as king forever.

Read Isaiah 9:6–7. How is the heir to David's throne described in verse 6?

_____

What titles would the child carry (v. 6)? _____

_____

Some fourteen generations later, a young virgin woman who lived in a town named Nazareth received a startling visit from an angel named Gabriel. Let's see what message Gabriel had to deliver to the young woman. Read Luke 1:26–35.

Who was Joseph's ancestor (v. 27)? _____

What name was Mary to give the child to be born (v. 31)? _____

What would He be called according to verse 32? _____

What throne would God give Him, and how long was He to reign?

Take a moment to read about the child's birth in Luke 2:1–15.

In what familiar town did Mary give birth to Jesus (v. 4)?

By what two titles did the angels call Jesus in verse 11?

Now let's pull all of this together. What key people from our study appear in Jesus's list of ancestors in Matthew 1:5?

The Wonderful Counselor, Mighty God, Prince of Peace, Son of the Most High God, Savior, and Messiah was the adopted son of Joseph, a descendant of David and the grandson of the servant named Obed, who was born from the blessed union of Boaz and Ruth. What a glorious ending to Ruth's story. But the greatest takeaway Ruth's story offers us is the realization that the same God who orchestrated all those generations of details and unions is also at work in our lives today.

> . . . the same God who orchestrated all those generations of details and unions is also at work in our lives today.

WEEK SIX DAY THREE

Behold A New Life

Therefore, if anyone is in Christ, he is a new creation. The old has passed away; behold, the new has come.

2 CORINTHIANS 5:17 (ESV)

Boaz and Ruth were married, and the Lord granted them the blessing of a son. All the labels of Ruth's past were behind her, and she became a part of the Israelite community there in Bethlehem. She had a new name, a new home, and a new son. Everything about Ruth's life had changed. Her old life was gone, and her new life had begun. As I consider all the newness of Ruth's life there in Bethlehem, 2 Corinthians 5:17 keeps running through my mind. Read it at the top of the page.

My favorite word in the whole verse is *behold*. In fact, I think it should have an exclamation point as well as those little lines coming from it that we place in drawings to depict light. You can picture it now too, right?

Either online or in a dictionary, look up the word *behold*. Write the definition below:

_____

_____

The definition you found probably says something about observing someone or something remarkable. The emphasis on observing something remarkable is what I want to highlight today with the word *behold*.

Ruth was a widow, but *behold*, she is now the wife of Boaz.

Ruth was a foreigner who wasn't part of the Israelite family, but *behold*, she is now the wife of Boaz—a man of standing in Bethlehem.

Ruth was poor and needy, but *behold*, she now enjoys the harvests from a great plot of land.

Ruth was barren, but *behold*, she now has a son.

God did some amazing work in Ruth's life, and every aspect of that work is cause for celebration. Her circumstances were dramatically and wonderfully changed. But there is another fact we can behold about Ruth's new life that has eternal implications for her then as well as for us today.

Ruth 2:12 is the focus passage for our study. Just to cement the concept in your heart, write that verse on the lines below.

_____

_____

Ruth found refuge under God's wings (*kanaph*), and His providential care was then evident in every aspect of her life. Her new life is truly something to behold. As believers in Jesus, we have also found refuge under the blessed covering of God's *kanaph* (Ruth 2:12), and there is another 2:12 passage in the Bible that helps us better understand exactly how the story of Ruth's new life correlates to our own faith stories.

Now, this is going to be a fragmented thought, but write Ephesians 2:12 below.

_____

_____

Let's look at the context for verse 12. According to Ephesians 2:11, who are those that "were separate from Christ, excluded from citizenship in Israel and foreigners to the covenants of the promise, without hope and without God in the world"?

_____

A simple definition of Gentile is a non-Jew (or non-Israelite). Ruth was a Gentile. The description in verse 12 sounds a lot like her, doesn't it? She was a Moabite, "excluded from citizenship in Israel" and a foreigner. She was formerly "without God" in her Moabite world.

Look back at Ruth 1:16, and focus on Ruth's words to Naomi as you fill in the blanks below.

". . . your people will be my _____ and your God _____."

Look again at Ruth 2:12. How is the Lord described? _____

When Ruth made the decision to return to Bethlehem with Naomi, she didn't just relocate. Ruth decided to place her faith in the Lord, the God of Israel, and become a part of the people of Israel. Now, hang with me. We will tie this together by the end of this lesson. But we need to gather the necessary information to put these concepts together. Read Deuteronomy 7:6.

> Ruth decided to place her faith in the Lord, the God of Israel, and become a part of the people of Israel.

In what two ways does God (through Moses) describe the people of Israel in verse 6?

1). _____

2). _____

In ancient Israel, anyone who was not a descendant of an Israelite was called a Gentile. God chose Israel to be "holy to the Lord," which means they were set apart for His purposes. Of all the nations on earth, Israel was chosen as God's treasured possession. Our Lord had special work He was going to do through the people of Israel.

Now, turn back to Ephesians 2 and read verses 11–18.

How have those who were once far away been brought near to God (v. 13)?

_____

_____

What two groups were brought together to make one humanity that is reconciled to God?

_____

_____

How were both Gentiles and Israelites reconciled to God (v. 16)?

_____

_____

Through faith in Jesus, both Jews (Israelites) and Gentiles have been reconciled to God, covered by God's *kanaph* by the blessed blood of Jesus, have access to God the Father through the death of God the Son (Jesus), and are united by God the Spirit. That was the work God chose to do through the nation of Israel—the birth and death of Jesus, the Messiah, who would reconcile all people to God through the shedding of His blood on the cross.

Now read Acts 3:24–25. Who did God say He would bless through Abraham?

_____

According to Ephesians 2:8, how are both Jews and Gentiles saved?

_____

According to Galatians 3:7–9, what did God announce to Abraham in advance?

_____

What did Jesus say about Abraham in John 8:56? _____

God announced His plan to send His Son, Jesus—the Christ (which means Messiah)—to save both Jews and Gentiles. All who believed in Him would be reconciled to God. Abraham probably didn't understand all that the coming Messiah would suffer, but He believed God would accomplish His work of reconciling the world to Himself through Abraham's descendant—the Messiah, who we know is our Jesus. Abraham and his descendants placed their faith in the coming Messiah. Christians place our faith in the risen Messiah. Through faith in Jesus as that long-anticipated Messiah, Jews and Gentiles alike are reconciled to God. Let's look at one final passage of Scripture together today. Read Galatians 3:26–29.

What do you learn about everyone who places their faith in the Messiah, Jesus?

_____

Our life before we find refuge in Christ doesn't matter. We are new creations. We are all children of God. We are all heirs to God's precious promises. I would say that is undoubtedly a remarkable truth to *behold*.

WEEK SIX · DAY FOUR

Under His Wings

The LORD reigns, let the nations tremble; he sits enthroned between the cherubim, let the earth shake.

PSALM 99:1

Ruth found refuge under God's *kanaph*. Boaz was her kinsman-redeemer, but ultimately, it was the Lord's redeeming love that enabled her to become a part of God's chosen people—His treasured possession. Israel was set apart for God's glorious purpose of bringing about the Messiah who would save not only the nation of Israel, but also the Gentiles—which consists of people from all other nations (Genesis 12:3). Through Jesus, all who choose to believe in God's divine plan for salvation are considered one big family of God. His love and His grace are available to everyone who chooses to accept Jesus as Savior. Some people consider Christianity exclusive, but I have always struggled to understand that perspective, because I consider His offer of salvation through faith to be beautifully inclusive. Anyone, regardless of background or ethnicity, can be saved through faith in Jesus. Not only that, but our Lord didn't exclusively use Israelites to carry out His plan of salvation.

Look again at the lineage of Christ that is recorded in Matthew 1, and focus on verse 5. What two Gentiles from Ruth's story were incorporated into God's providential plan to bring about the Savior of the world?

God not only allowed Ruth to find refuge under His wings, He allowed her the privilege of participating in His divine plan. Considering Rahab's former occupation (Joshua 6:17) and the utter depravity of the Moabite culture of which Ruth was a part, their participation in His divine work is an example of unfathomable grace (giving us what we don't deserve) and mercy (withholding what we do deserve). God's plan of salvation seems mercifully inclusive to me.

As we finalize our study, I want to focus your attention once again on what it means to find refuge under God's *kanaph*. I have saved this lesson for today, mostly because I feel inadequate to explain it. So, I am going start by directing you to another 2:12 passage.

Read 1 Corinthians 2:11–12. According to verse 12, what does the Spirit help us do?

_____

Take a minute to ask the Spirit to grant you understanding as we work through what could be a complicated lesson.

Did you pray? Okay, then I trust the Spirit to do His work. Let's dive right in.

After our Lord rescued His people from slavery in Egypt, He instructed Moses to build a large tent structure called the *tabernacle*, which was eventually upgraded to a temple by King Solomon. It was a place where the people worshiped, and Moses met with God. Among the holy furnishings the people made for the temple, there was a wooden box covered in pure gold that was called the Ark of the Covenant. It held sacred items including the tablets of stone on which God wrote the Ten Commandments. (Remember the ones Moses had to chisel himself after he broke the original tablets?) Once the Ark was completed, a cover was created for the it. That cover will be the focus of our lesson today.

Begin by reading Exodus 25:17–21. Give a general description of the cover.

_____

_____

What was the name for the cover (v. 17)? _____

What was overshadowing the cover (v. 20)?

_____

The word *wings* in Exodus 25:20 is the Hebrew word *kanaph*. Now read Exodus 25:22, and note where the Lord met with Moses.

_____

How are the Lord's meetings with Moses described in Exodus 33:11?

_____

When Ruth took refuge under God's wings (Ruth 2:12), I would like to suggest it was a reference to the wings of the cherubim that were overshadowing the atonement cover of the Ark. A *kanaph*, whether describing the wings of the cherubim or the edges of an Israelite's outer garment, which were a reminder of the cherubim's wings, is a place where God's people find refuge in His holy presence. Under His *kanaph*, we can speak with Him "as one speaks to a friend" (Exodus 33:11).

According to 2 Chronicles 5:7–8, where in the tabernacle (or later the temple) was the Ark of the Covenant located?

_____

What clue do you find in Psalm 99:1 about why the innermost sanctuary where the Ark of the Covenant was kept was named the Most Holy Place?

_____

Stay with me. I want you to look up all these verses so you can put all of this together yourself. What does Hebrews 8:5 tell you about the layout of the tabernacle?

_____

Our Lord is enthroned between the cherubim in His heavenly dwelling, and when we find refuge in His redeeming love, we can rest in His holy presence and enjoy sweet fellowship with the One who created us and knows everything past, present, and future. He is aware of the matters that weigh heavily on your heart here on earth. He allows you to find refuge in His holy presence.

> He is aware of the matters that weigh heavily on your heart here on earth.

To finish today, take a moment to talk to our Lord like one speaks with a friend. You are safe in His presence. Share your fears, your joys, your struggles, and your hopes, just as you would tell a trusted friend. Jot down your thoughts or your prayers below. No lines this time. You are free in His presence.

Thoughts and Prayers

Redeeming Love

God so loved the world that he gave his one and only Son, that whoever believes in Him shall not perish but have eternal life.

JOHN 3:16

Yesterday, we focused on the atonement cover that covered the Ark of the Covenant, which was kept in the Most Holy Place of the tabernacle (later the temple). That sanctuary and its components were simply "a copy and shadow of what is in heaven" (Hebrews 8:5). The Ark was reflective of God's heavenly throne room where He is "enthroned between the cherubim" (Psalm 99:1). It is under His wings (*kanaph*) that we find refuge in His Holy presence. He is our refuge. He is our safe place, He cares for us and is faithful to accomplish His purposes in us and through us. Our God allows us the unfathomable privilege of speaking to Him as one speaks with his friend (Exodus 33:11). I hope you took time to do just that as we ended yesterday's lesson.

Today I want to continue applying and broadening our understanding of what Scripture teaches about the refuge we find in God's presence because of His redeeming love expressed through the death of His Son.

Look back at yesterday's lesson. In what area of the earthly sanctuary was the Ark of the Covenant kept?

Begin today by reading Exodus 26:30–34.

What divided the Holy Place from the Most Holy Place where God's presence dwelled?

The thick curtain (also called a *veil*) that shielded the Ark from the other areas of the sanctuary was made of yarn and twisted linen. No one except the high priest was allowed into God's presence behind the veil, and even the high priest was only allowed to enter the Most Holy Place once per year on the Day of Atonement. A simple definition for *atonement* is "the act of being reconciled to God." I remember its meaning by breaking up the word *atonement* into syllables and pronouncing it "at-one-ment." The purpose of the high priest's offerings was to atone (or make restitution for) the people's sins. The blood of innocent goats and lambs was offered to temporarily reconcile or make the people "at one" with God.

Once again, this has the potential to be a complicated final lesson.

Read Hebrews 9:1–7.

What did the high priest offer to atone for himself and the sins of the people? _____

Read Hebrews 9:8–12.

According to verse 10, what was the purpose of the gifts and sacrifices offered in the earthly sanctuaries?

_____

In what tabernacle did Jesus enter the Most Holy Place (v. 11)?

_____

Whose blood did He offer? _____

According to verse 12, what was gained? _____

Every year on the Day of Atonement, a high priest would go behind the veil into the Most Holy Place of the tabernacle to sprinkle the blood of innocent animals on the Ark to atone for the sins of the people. Those sacrifices reconciled the people to God temporarily, but they could not clear their consciences from the guilt for their sins (Hebrews 9:9). They were simply annual reminders of sin (Hebrews 10:3).

Now read Hebrews 9:19–26.

What is required for forgiveness (v. 22)? _____

According to verse 24, what sanctuary did Jesus enter, and what does He do for us?

_____

One last passage brings these thoughts together.

Read Matthew 27:45–54. What happened at the temple the moment Jesus died?

_____

The earthly sanctuaries were representative of the true heavenly sanctuary in which the presence of God dwells. The annual sacrifices required for the high priests to enter God's presence and atone for the people's sins were only representations of the true sacrifice in which Jesus shed His blood to bring forgiveness for all sins for all time. He entered God's throne room in heaven itself (Hebrews 9:24), and His sacrifice not only atones for the sins of all people who place their faith in Him, it tore the veil that prevented our access to His presence. Jesus is our high priest forever (Hebrews 5:6), and His sacrifice covers our sins for all time.

Read Hebrews 4:14–16.

Other than His status of eternal high priest, what else is distinctive about Jesus (v. 15)?

_____

Jesus not only has been tempted in every way we have, which means he can sympathize with our weaknesses, but He never gave in to those temptations and is perfect and sinless. Those innocent calves and goats shed their blood to impress upon the people that innocent blood must be shed to cover the sins of the guilty. Jesus obtained "eternal redemption" (Hebrews 9:12) for everyone who believes in Him. His innocent blood was shed to cover the guilty.

Read John 3:16–18.

What was the motivation for God to send His son to shed His blood to gain eternal redemption for you and for me (v. 16)?

_____

WEEK SIX

119

God's love compelled Him to send Jesus to be our eternal Redeemer. Through His shed blood we are granted merciful forgiveness and everlasting life in His glorious presence. We not only find refuge in His redeeming love while on this earth, but when our days here are complete, we will enjoy the security of refuge in His holy presence for all time.

Through faith, Ruth found refuge under God's wings, and God's providential care was evident throughout her life. Ruth's story helps us better understand our stories. The greatest expression of God's providential care for His people was when He sent His Son to show the world the depth of His redeeming love.

> Ruth's story helps us better understand our stories.

I loved studying this material with you, my friend.

May you be richly rewarded by the LORD,

the God of Israel, under whose wings

you have come to take refuge. (Ruth 2:12b)

NOTES

1. F. LaGard Smith, *The Narrated Bible in Chronological Order* (Eugene, OR: Harvest House Publishers, 1984), 365.
2. John F. Woolvoord and Roy B. Zuck, *The Bible Knowledge Commentary: An Exposition of the Scriptures by Dallas Seminary Faculty: Old Testament* (Colorado Springs: Cook Communications, 2000), 481.
3. Ralph Gower, *The New Manners and Customs of Bible Times* (Chicago: Moody Bible Institute of Chicago, 2000), 72.
4. Kenneth L. Barker and John R. Kohlenberger III, *The Expositor's Bible Commentary—Abridged Edition: Old Testament* (Grand Rapids, MI: Zondervan, 1994), 368.
5. Barker and Kohlenberger, *The Expositor's Bible Commentary*, 369.
6. Herbert Lockyer, *All the MEN of the Bible* (Grand Rapids, MI: Zondervan, 1958), 104.
7. Daniel I. Block, *The New American Commentary*, vol. 6, *Judges, Ruth* (Nashville: B&H Publishing Group, 1999), 60.
8. Smith, *The Narrated Bible in Chronological Order*, 365.
9. Adele Berlin and Marc Zvi Brettler, *The Jewish Study Bible: Featuring the Jewish Publication Society TANAKH Translation* (New York: Oxford University Press, 2004), 517.
10. Block, *The New American Commentary*, vol. 6, *Judges, Ruth*, 632.
11. Block, *The New American Commentary*, vol. 6, *Judges, Ruth*, 682.
12. John F. Walvoord and Roy B. Zuck, *The Bible Knowledge Commentary: Old Testament* (Colorado Springs: Cook Communications Ministries, 1983), 307.
13. Berlin and Brettler, *The Jewish Study Bible*, 422–23.
14. Walvoord and Zuck, *The Bible Knowledge Commentary: Old Testament*, 421.
15. Walvoord and Zuck, *The Bible Knowledge Commentary: Old Testament*, 421.
16. Merrill C. Tenney, *New International Bible Dictionary* (Grand Rapids, MI: Zondervan, 1987), 796.
17. Eugene H. Merrill, *The Bible Knowledge Word Study: Joshua–2 Chronicles* (Colorado Springs: Cook Communications Ministries, 2004), 117.
18. Lockyer, *All the MEN of the Bible*, 79.
19. Herbert Lockyer, *All the WOMEN of the Bible* (Grand Rapids, MI: Zondervan, 1967), 130.
20. Block, *The New American Commentary*, vol. 6, *Judges, Ruth*, 665.
21. Gower, *The New Manners and Customs of Bible Times*, 78.
22. Gower, *The New Manners and Customs of Bible Times*, 80.
23. Block, *The New American Commentary*, vol. 6, *Judges, Ruth*, 670.
24. Barker, Kenneth L. and Kohlenberger III, John R. *The Expositor's Bible Commentary—Abridged Edition: Old Testament*, Zondervan Corporation, 1994, 373.
25. Merrill, *The Bible Knowledge Word Study: Joshua–2 Chronicles*, 114.
26. Berlin and Brettler, *The Jewish Study Bible*, 1583.
27. Block, *The New American Commentary*, vol. 6, *Judges, Ruth*, 684.
28. Block, *The New American Commentary*, vol. 6, *Judges, Ruth*, 685.

29. J. I. Packer and M. C. Tenny, *Illustrated Manners and Customs of the Bible: Nelson's Super Value Series* (Nashville: Thomas Nelson, 1980), 480.

30. Merrill, *The Bible Knowledge Word Study: Joshua–2 Chronicles*, 118.

31. Merriam-Webster.com Dictionary, s.v. "Refuge," accessed November 4, 2022, www.merriam-webster.com /dictionary/refuge.

32. Merrill, *The Bible Knowledge Word Study: Joshua–2 Chronicles*, 119.

33. Lawrence O. Richards, *New International Encyclopedia of Bible Words: Based on the NIV and the NASB* (Grand Rapids, MI: Zondervan, 1991), 516–17.

34. M. G. Easton *Illustrated Bible Dictionary*, 3rd ed., s.v. "Goodness of God" (Edinburgh: Thomas Nelson, 1897), paragraph 3093.

35. Joyce Baldwin, "Ruth," in *New Bible Commentary*, 21st Century Edition, Accordance electronic ed., ed. D. A. Carson et al. (Downers Grove, IL: InterVarsity Press, 1994), 291–92, https://accordance.bible/link/read/IVP -NB_Commentary#3663.

36. W. Hall Harris, ed., *The NET Bible Notes*, 2nd ed. (Nashville: Thomas Nelson, 2019), paragraph 19250, https://accordance.bible/link/read/NET_Notes#19250.

37. Block, *The New American Commentary*, vol. 6, *Judges, Ruth*, 704–5.

38. Merrill, *The Bible Knowledge Word Study: Joshua–2 Chronicles*120.

39. Block, *The New American Commentary*, vol. 6, *Judges, Ruth*, 706.

40. Berlin and Brettler. *The Jewish Study Bible*, 1584.

41. Block, *The New American Commentary*, vol. 6, *Judges, Ruth*, 710.

42. Harris, ed., *The NET Bible*, 501.

43. Block, *The New American Commentary*, vol. 6, *Judges, Ruth*, 725.

44. Gower, *New Manners and Customs of Bible Times*, 56.

45. Alfred J. Kolatch, *The Jewish Book of Why* (Middle Village, NY: Jonathan David Publishers, 1981), 36.

46. Gower, *The New Manners and Customs of Bible Times*, 56.

47. Kolatch, *The Jewish Book of Why*, 35.

48. Kolatch, *The Jewish Book of Why*, 35.

49. Kolatch, *The Jewish Book of Why*, 35.

50. Kolatch, *The Jewish Book of Why*, 36.

51. Packer and Tenny, *Illustrated Manners and Customs of the Bible*, 481.

52. Packer and Tenny, *Illustrated Manners and Customs of the Bible*, 481.

53. Kolatch*The Jewish Book of Why*, 22.

54. William Whiston, *Josephus: The Complete Works: The Antiquities of the Jews*, 5.9.3 (Nashville: Thomas Nelson Publishers, 1998), 177.

WALKING HAND IN HAND AS CHRIST'S LOVE
transforms lives

AMG
INTERNATIONAL

MEETING THE
DEEPEST NEEDS

WE BELIEVE THE GOSPEL IS TRANSFORMATIVE

And you can change the world one child at a time.

Thousands of children in the world are born into a cycle of poverty that has been around for generations, leaving them without hope for a safe and secure future. For a little more than $1 a day you can provide the tools a child needs to break the cycle in the name of Jesus.

OUR CONTACT

📞 423-894-6060

✉️ info@amginternational.org

📷 @amgintl

📍 6815 Shallowford Rd. Chattanooga, TN 37421

Made in the USA
Middletown, DE
21 June 2023

32551271R00075